Asperger Syndrome

Asperger Syndrome

A Guide for Parents and Educators

SECOND EDITION

Brenda Smith Myles
Richard L. Simpson

pro·ed
An International Publisher

8700 Shoal Creek Boulevard
Austin, Texas 78757-6897
800/897-3202 Fax 800/397-7633
www.proedinc.com

© 1998, 2003 by PRO-ED, Inc.
8700 Shoal Creek Boulevard
Austin, Texas 78757-6897
800/897-3202   Fax 800/397-7633
www.proedinc.com

Library of Congress Cataloging–in–Publication Data

Myles, Brenda.
    Asperger syndrome : a guide for educators and parents / Brenda Smith Myles,
    Richard L. Simpson—2nd ed.
        p. cm.
    Includes bibliographical references and index.
    ISBN 0-89079-898-2
        1. Asperger's syndrome—Patients—Family relationships. 2. Parents of autistic
    children. 3. Autistic children—Family relationships. 4. Autistic children—
    Education. 5. Children—Mental health. I. Simpson, Richard L., 1945– II. Title.

RJ506.A9 M95 2003
616.89'82–dc21

2002069867

This book is designed in Italia and New Century Schoolbook.

Printed in the United States of America

3   4   5   6   7   8   9   10   06   05

Contents

Preface

It was more than 5 decades ago that the Viennese psychiatrist Hans Asperger published a seminal paper wherein he described a group of children with a unique social disability (Asperger, 1944). The disorder he described continues to be known by his name—Asperger Syndrome. For decades the term was primarily used in certain sections of Europe, with virtually no mention in the United States. Times have changed. Currently *Asperger Syndrome* is used worldwide to describe individuals with significant social and language peculiarities who simultaneously reveal normal development and functioning in some areas of their lives. Indeed, there has been a dramatic increase over the past several years in the number of children and youth identified as having Asperger Syndrome.

In spite of the exponential increase in the diagnostic use of the term *Asperger Syndrome* in the United States and Canada, and the predictable interest among parents, family members, and professionals, there is an enormous lack of understanding regarding the disorder. This lack of understanding is directly related to lack of information about the disability, including its relationship to other "autistic-like" conditions. It is clear that parents and professionals alike are struggling to learn more about Asperger Syndrome, especially about effective methods for assisting children and youth diagnosed with the disability. Unfortunately, there are few resources available to satisfy the growing demand for information about Asperger Syndrome.

This need for basic information about Asperger Syndrome is the foundation of this book. We wanted to write a book that would be easily understood by both professionals and laypeople; that would address basic issues related to the characteristics of children and youth with the disorder; and that would outline basic methods to facilitate the growth and development of children and youth with Asperger Syndrome in the home, school, and community.

This book consists of six chapters. Chapter 1 provides an overview of Asperger Syndrome, including definitions and characteristics. Chapter 2 focuses on educational assessment and planning for students with Asperger Syndrome. Chapter 3 addresses basic academic support measures, and Chapter 4 focuses on behavior management methods appropriate for children and youth with Asperger Syndrome. Chapter 5 offers information and suggestions for social skills instruction and enhancement. Finally, Chapter 6 explores the impact of Asperger Syndrome on families. This final chapter is authored by several parents who chose not to identify themselves by name. Each of the chapters is written in a straightforward style. The book contains minimal review of research; references are included only where required. Although there are potential problems with this strategy, we adopted it in an effort to make the book user-friendly and readable.

This book bears the names of only two authors. However, there were a number of people involved in its development. Our colleague Judith K. Carlson, PhD, offered suggestions and input on several chapters. Laura B. Carpenter, EdD, contributed the section on developing and using a travel card. Valerie Janke Rexin, MS, Elisa Gagnon, MS, Edna Smith, PhD, and Katherine Tapscott Cook, MS, were responsible for developing several examples in the book. Without the clerical support provided by Ginny Biddulph, this project would never have been brought to fruition. Finally, but in no way of least importance, we thank the children and youth with Asperger Syndrome and their parents who contributed information about their lives and their needs, for this was our inspiration.

Understanding Asperger Syndrome

In 1944 Hans Asperger, a Viennese physician, published his postgraduate thesis ("Autistic Psychopathy" in Childhood), wherein he described a group of children with a significant and chronic neurodevelopmental social disorder. Interest in this disability, known today as Asperger Syndrome, was slow to develop. Indeed, for decades little was written or known about Asperger Syndrome. Today, however, interest in Asperger Syndrome has dramatically increased, and the disorder is rapidly becoming a part of the everyday lexicon of parents, educators, and other professionals.

In his seminal work Asperger (1944) described four children with a propensity toward social isolation and awkwardness. In addition to social peculiarities, these children displayed a variety of "typical autistic behaviors," such as self-stimulatory responses and insistence on environmental sameness. However, unlike other children with autism, they generally had normal intellectual and language development, leading Asperger to infer that individuals with this disorder represented a distinct and independent diagnostic classification. Over time Asperger made changes in his original conceptualization of children with Asperger Syndrome. However, the essential clinical characteristics remained the same, leading researchers and writers such as Wing (1981), C. Gillberg (1989), Frith (1991), Volkmar, Klin, and Cohen (1997), and Klin, Volkmar, and Sparrow (2000) to conclude that Asperger's characterizations have withstood the test of time.

Over the past decade Asperger Syndrome has been increasingly recognized and experienced by professionals and parents. This exponential increase in interest and the corresponding increase in the number of individuals diagnosed with the disorder are directly correlated with recognition of Asperger Syndrome as a subclassification of pervasive developmental disorder in the widely used *Diagnostic and Statistical Manual of Mental Disorders–Fourth Edition* (DSM–IV; American Psychiatric Association, 1994) and the corresponding international classification system, *International Statistical Classification of Diseases and Related Health Problems* (10th ed.; ICD–10; World Health Organization, 1992). However, in spite of this ever-increasing interest, understanding of this disability lags significantly behind its recognition.

For example, there is significant confusion and lack of clarity related to the salient, defining, and unique characteristics of Asperger Syndrome. Lack of diagnostic reliability is another problem with the disorder. There is also debate on whether Asperger Syndrome is an independent diagnostic category or simply another dimension of the so-called autism spectrum. Indeed, there is enormous disagreement and lack of understanding regarding this disorder and its relationship to other "autistic-like" conditions. This chapter describes characteristics and other issues related to understanding the unique elements of Asperger Syndrome.

Diagnostic Classification of Asperger Syndrome

Asperger Syndrome has historically been connected with the more widely used term *autism* and more recently with *autism spectrum disorder.* Kanner's (1943) original description of children with autism (i.e., relationship difficulties, delayed speech and language development and other speech and language abnormalities, normal physical growth and development, insistence on environmental sameness, obsessive preoccupation with objects, and repetitive and other self-stimulatory responses) has served as a general blueprint for understanding individuals with Asperger Syndrome. Thus, individuals with the syndrome have often been thought of as being an upper element of the so-called autism spectrum.

As Kanner's original characteristics of autism have been revised and refined, so too have conceptualizations of Asperger Syndrome. That is, even though the professional community embraces basic elements of Hans Asperger's notions regarding Asperger Syndrome, nuances and minor amendments to the original conceptions of the disorder have occurred over the decades. This process of refining the characteristics of Asperger Syndrome was particularly stimulated by Wing (1981), who attempted to clarify and identify the disorder through extensive clinical descriptions and case examples. Others have also contributed to an increased understanding of Asperger Syndrome, including similarities and differences between it and other autism conditions and diagnostic criteria for the syndrome (C. L. Gillberg, 1992; I. C. Gillberg & Gillberg, 1989; Klin, Volkmar, & Sparrow, 2000).

In the United States the most widely used diagnostic criteria for Asperger Syndrome are included in the *Diagnostic and Statistical Manual of Mental Disorders–Fourth Edition–Text Revision* (DSM–IV–TR; American Psychiatric Association, 2000). This diagnostic and clinical manual classifies Asperger Syndrome as one of five pervasive developmental disorders. According to the DSM–IV–TR, *pervasive developmental disorder* is used in reference to persons who are "characterized by severe and pervasive impairment in several areas of development: reciprocal social interaction skills, communication skills, or the presence of stereotyped behavior, interests, and activities" (p. 69). Other pervasive developmental disorders are identified in the DSM–IV–TR: autistic disorder, childhood disintegrative disorder, Rett's disorder, and pervasive development disorder–not otherwise specified. A summary of DSM–IV–TR diagnostic criteria for Asperger Syndrome is shown in Table 1.1.

The international counterpart of the DSM–IV–TR is the ICD–10 (World Health Organization, 1992). This classification also uses the term *pervasive developmental disorders* to refer to autism spectrum disorders, and conceptualizes and defines autism similarly to the DSM–IV–TR. That is, it includes and similarly defines the following specific disorders: Asperger Syndrome, childhood autism, Rett's syndrome, other childhood

Table 1.1
DSM–IV–TR Diagnostic Criteria for Asperger Syndrome

A. Qualitative impairment in social interaction, as manifested by at least two of the following:

1. Significant impairment in nonverbal behavior use, including social interaction gestures, facial expression, eye-to-eye contact, and body postures.

2. Inability to form and maintain developmentally appropriate relationships with peers.

3. Failure to spontaneously seek out others for interactions, including sharing interests, enjoyment, or achievements.

4. Difficulty with social or emotional reciprocity.

B. Repetitive and restricted stereotyped patterns of behavior, activities, and interests, as shown by at least one of the following:

1. Significant preoccupation with one or more stereotyped and restricted interest patterns whose focus or intensity makes it abnormal.

2. Significant display of nonfunctional routines or inflexible adherence to rituals.

3. Repetitive and stereotyped motor movements such as complex whole-body movements, or hand or finger flapping or twisting.

4. Significant and persistent preoccupation with parts of objects.

C. Clinically significant social, occupational, or other impairment in functioning.

D. Absence of a clinically significant general language delay.

E. Absence of a clinically significant delay in cognitive development or in development of age-appropriate adaptive behavior (other than social interaction), self-help skills, and childhood curiosity about the environment.

F. Failure to meet diagnostic criteria for schizophrenia or another pervasive developmental disorder.

Note. Adapted from the *Diagnostic and Statistical Manual of Mental Disorders–Fourth Edition–Text Revision* (p. 84), by American Psychiatric Association, 2000, Washington, DC: Author. Copyright 2000 by the American Psychiatric Association. Adapted with permission.

disintegrative disorders, other pervasive developmental disorders, pervasive developmental disorders–unspecified, overactive disorder with mental retardation with stereotyped movements, and atypical autism.

Description of Children and Youth with Asperger Syndrome

Children and youth with Asperger Syndrome share characteristics with children and youth with autism, as originally described by Kanner (1943), but Asperger Syndrome also has a number of unique features. Clinical features of Asperger Syndrome include abnormalities or deficits in social interaction; in speech and communication, cognitive, academic and learning, and sensory characteristics; and in physical and motor skills.

Social Interaction Impairments

Children and youth with Asperger Syndrome demonstrate social deficits and peculiarities that continue into adulthood. Indeed, the DSM–IV–TR notes that "the impairment in reciprocal social interaction is gross and sustained" (p. 80). Many such children and adolescents appear to be interested in interacting with others; however, their interactions tend to be inept or characterized by inability to engage in age-expected social interactions, including appropriate play. Indeed, the social deficits of children and adolescents with Asperger Syndrome may be due more to lack of understanding of appropriate social customs than to disinterest or fear of social contact. For example, a child with Asperger Syndrome may appear rude or odd because he seems unwilling to take turns in play and conversation or to understand a peer's subtle social cues, in spite of his willingness to seek out others on the playground.

In accordance with these behavioral patterns, children and youth with Asperger Syndrome can fall anywhere from withdrawn to active on the behavioral continuum. That is, they can be expected to range from being socially reclusive and preferring isolation to being socially outgoing and interested in having regular contact with others. Regardless of where they fit on this spectrum, however, they are routinely viewed as socially awkward, socially stiff, emotionally blunted, self-centered, unable to understand nonverbal social cues, inflexible, and lacking in empathy and understanding. Therefore, even when children and adolescents with Asperger Syndrome actively try to seek out others, they encounter social isolation because of their lack of understanding of the rules of social behavior, including eye contact, proximity to others, gestures, posture, and so forth.

In one of the few studies that attempted to identify the nature of behavior problems and adaptive behavior among students with Asperger Syndrome, Barnhill, Hagiwara, Myles, Simpson, et al. (2000) compared behavior rating scale inventories completed by parents, teachers, and students. Results revealed that parents had significantly greater concern about the behavior and social skills of their children than did the students' teachers. Responses also revealed that parents perceived their children to have clinically significant problems in a variety of socially related areas, including overall behavioral problems, such as conduct problems, aggression, and hyperactivity, as well as internalizing problems, such as withdrawal. In contrast, teachers perceived the children and adolescents in the study to have both fewer and less significant problems than did parents, although they did view the children to be "at risk" in the areas of anxiety, depression, attention problems, and withdrawal. Students' self-evaluations revealed that they did not perceive themselves to have significant problems or to be at risk on any of the clinical components of the scale.

It is not unusual for individuals with Asperger Syndrome to be able to engage in routine social interactions (e.g., greetings) without being able to engage in extended interactions or two-way relationships. Thus, children and youth with Asperger Syndrome are commonly described by families and schoolmates as lacking awareness of social convention and protocol, lacking common sense, tending to misinterpret social cues and unspoken messages, and being inclined to display a variety of socially unaccepted and nonreciprocal responses.

It is also common for individuals with Asperger Syndrome to become emotionally vulnerable and easily stressed. For example, children with Asperger Syndrome may become agitated if they think others are invading their private space when they are in a crowded room or when they find themselves in the midst of several simultaneous social activities. However, unlike many normally developing and achieving peers, many children with Asperger Syndrome do not reveal stress through voice tone, body posture, and so forth. As a result, their agitation may escalate to a point of crisis because of others' unawareness of their discomfort, along with their own inability to monitor and control uncomfortable situations. Given these deficits, it is not surprising that children and youth with Asperger Syndrome are relatively easy targets for peers prone to teasing and bullying.

In spite of their frequent lack of social awareness, many individuals with Asperger Syndrome are aware that they are different from their peers. Thus, self-esteem problems, self-faultfinding, and self-deprecation are common among individuals with Asperger Syndrome.

Not surprisingly, many individuals with Asperger Syndrome are poor incidental social learners; that is, they tend to learn social skills without fully understanding their meaning and context. Indeed, many of these individuals attempt to rigidly and broadly follow universal social rules, because doing so provides structure to an otherwise confusing world. Unfortunately, this is often not a successful strategy because there are few, if any, universal and inflexible social rules. Yet, as any parent or teacher can attest, social relationships are extremely important for persons with Asperger Syndrome because they facilitate development of self-control and self-knowledge as well as use of functional language and related skills needed for day-to-day functioning.

Although behavioral problems are not universal among individuals with Asperger Syndrome, they are not uncommon. These problems often involve feelings of stress, fatigue, or loss of control or inability to predict outcomes. Thus, children with Asperger Syndrome do not have typical conduct problems, but rather behavioral problems connected to their inability to function in a world they see as unpredictable and threatening. Accordingly, there is little support for Asperger's (1944) original description of children with Asperger Syndrome as malicious and mean-spirited. Rather, when persons with the syndrome do experience behavioral difficulties, their problems are more likely caused by social ineptness, an obsessive and single-minded pursuit of a particular interest, or a defensive panic reaction.

As individuals with Asperger Syndrome age, more critical social and emotional problems often develop. Studies of adolescents (Cesaroni & Garber, 1991; Ghaziuddin, Weidmer-Mikhail, & Ghaziuddin, 1998) have indicated that these individuals experience heightened discomfort or anxiety in social situations, along with a continuing limited ability to interact with peers.

Wing (1981) noted that it is at this time that diagnosable depression and anxiety occur. Indeed, clinical reports have revealed that adolescents and young adults with Asperger Syndrome appear to be at risk for depression (Barnhill, 2001; Ghaziuddin et al., 1998).

Speech and Communication Characteristics

Unlike children with autism, those with Asperger Syndrome typically do not manifest clinically significant delays in language. Although there may be minimal language problems in some children with Asperger Syndrome, they typically tend to acquire and use words and phrases in accordance with expected developmental norms. In this regard, Frith (1991) observed that children with Asperger Syndrome "tend to speak fluently by the time they are five" (p. 3). However, she also observed that their language is frequently "odd in its use for communication" (p. 3). Wing (1981) reported that many individuals with Asperger Syndrome display a variety of communication deficits as infants and that many of their perceived "special abilities" could be explained as rote responses rather than normal or precocious language development.

It should be apparent from this discussion that there is disagreement among professionals regarding the extent to which children diagnosed with Asperger Syndrome display language acquisition delays and deficits (American Psychiatric Association, 2000; Wetherby & Prizant, 2000). However, there is no debate that children with Asperger Syndrome manifest a variety of abnormal communication characteristics, particularly in their social, conversational, and related skills (e.g., abnormal voice quality, monotonic voice). Thus, their often egocentric conversational style, one-sided monologues, and narrowly focused interests are independent of their early acquisition and use of words. For example, a child may repeat the same phrase over and over, talk with exaggerated inflections or in a monotone voice, discuss at length a single topic that is of little interest to others, or have difficulty sustaining conversation unless it focuses on a particular, narrowly defined topic. That there are communication problems associated with these patterns is not surprising, given that effective communication requires that individuals have shared topics and be willing to listen as well as talk. The adult-like, pedantic speaking style of some children with Asperger Syndrome may further lessen their appeal to their peers.

As might be expected, nonverbal communication deficits and related social communication problems are common among persons with Asperger Syndrome. These include problems during interactions, such as standing closer to another person than is customarily accepted; intensely staring at another person for long periods; maintaining abnormal body posture; failing to make eye contact or displaying an inexpressive face, thereby failing to signal interest, approval, or disapproval; and failing to use or understand gestures and facial expressions.

In school, students with Asperger Syndrome frequently have difficulty comprehending descriptions of abstract concepts; understanding and correctly using figures of speech such as metaphors, idioms, parables, and allegories; and grasping the meaning and intent of rhetorical questions. Because these conventions are commonly used by teachers and authors of school texts, deficits in this area have a negative effect on these students' academic success.

Cognitive Characteristics

A salient and defining characteristic of Asperger Syndrome is average or above-average intellectual capacity. Thus, both the ICD–10 (World Health Organization, 1992) and the DSM–IV–TR (American Psychiatric Association, 2000) note that a diagnosis of Asperger Syndrome is generally contingent upon an individual's not having a global cognitive deficit. However, in spite of this assumption and the recognition of the importance of cognitive profiles in understanding and planning for learners, relatively little is known about the cognitive and intellectual abilities of persons diagnosed with Asperger Syndrome. Indeed, many assumptions regarding the intellectual and cognitive characteristics of children and youth with Asperger Syndrome are based on studies of individuals with high-functioning autism. In this regard, several researchers have reported an uneven cognitive profile pattern on the Wechsler intelligence scales (Wechsler, 1989, 1991) among individuals with high-functioning autism, including Performance IQ scores that are significantly higher than Verbal IQ scores (Ehlers et al., 1997; Lincoln, Courchesne, Kilman, Elmasian, & Allen, 1988).

More specifically, individuals with high-functioning autism also obtained their highest scores on the Block Design subtest and their lowest scores on the Comprehension subtest. The Block Design element of the Wechsler intelligence scales is a nonverbal concept formation task that requires perceptual organization, spatial visualization, and abstract conceptualization and is believed to be a good measure of general intelligence. In contrast, the Comprehension subtest assesses an individual's understanding of social mores and interpersonal situations and is thus related to one's social judgment, common sense, and grasp of social conventionality. It is not surprising that individuals with autism spectrum disorders (including those with Asperger Syndrome) would be expected to score relatively poorly on a test designed to measure social comprehension. It is important to be cautious in making generalizations about the cognitive and intellectual characteristics of children with Asperger Syndrome, however, based on studies of individuals with high-functioning autism.

In one of the few studies of cognitive abilities of children and youth with Asperger Syndrome, Barnhill, Hagiwara, Myles, and Simpson (2000) assessed the cognitive profiles of 37 children and youth with Asperger Syndrome, as measured by the Wechsler scales (Wechsler, 1989, 1991). The scores generally fell within the average range of abilities, although the range of IQs was from intellectually deficient to very superior. No significant difference existed between the Verbal IQ and Performance IQ scores. Consistent with the findings of others, the study also revealed relatively high Block Design subtest scores, suggesting relatively strong nonverbal reasoning ability and visual–motor spatial integration. Relatively low scores were found on the Coding subtest, suggesting that many of the subjects had visual–motor coordination difficulties, were distractible, were disinterested in school-related tasks, and had visual memory weakness. The subjects also obtained relatively low scores on the Comprehension subtest, suggesting poor social judgment. It is important to note, however, that this and other studies have failed to identify a specific cognitive profile among individuals diagnosed with Asperger Syndrome.

Several theories have been proposed to explain the uneven cognitive performance of individuals with Asperger Syndrome. Among the most popular of these explanations is the one suggesting that individuals with Asperger Syndrome have a "theory of mind" deficit (Baron-Cohen, Leslie, & Frith, 1985). Theory of mind refers to individuals' ability to think about and use information related to their and others' intentions, beliefs, and mental states. Thus, in accordance with poor theory-of-mind capacity, a weakness in perspective taking and related abilities would explain at least some of the problems of individuals with Asperger Syndrome, as well as offer a plausible explanation for their irregular profile on certain types of IQ tests.

Academic and Learning Characteristics

In spite of their typically average intellectual abilities and ability to be included in general education classrooms, many students with Asperger Syndrome can be expected to experience academic performance problems. Indeed, social and communication deficits, in combination with obsessive and narrowly defined interests, concrete and literal thinking styles, inflexibility, poor problem-solving skills, poor organizational skills, difficulty in discerning relevant from irrelevant stimuli, and weak social standing, often make it difficult for students with Asperger Syndrome to fully participate in and comprehend general education curricula and instructional systems. Nevertheless, in spite of these challenges, many children and youth with Asperger Syndrome are able to attend college and have successful careers.

Some children and youth with Asperger Syndrome are thought to have learning disabilities (Frith, 1991; Siegel, Minshew, & Goldstein, 1996). In fact, this interpretation extends as far back as Asperger (1944) himself, who described the academic performance of the children with whom he worked as uneven. Moreover, as countless parents and teachers experience daily, Asperger observed that children with Asperger Syndrome, although highly verbal, often fail academic subjects that do not align with their special interests and obsessions.

Although strong empirical support is lacking, students with Asperger Syndrome are widely thought to experience problems related to comprehending abstract materials, metaphors, idioms, and other figures of speech; discriminating relevant from irrelevant information; and understanding inferentially based materials. Strengths among learners with Asperger Syndrome tend to be in comprehension of factual material (Church, Alisanski, &

Amanullah, 2000). A study of academic achievement undertaken by Griswold, Barnhill, Myles, Hagiwara, and Simpson (2002) revealed that although students' mean academic achievement scores fell within the average range, the scores ranged from significantly below average to significantly above average. Relative strengths were in the areas of oral expression and reading recognition. Students who participated in the study revealed relative weakness in the area of listening comprehension (i.e., comprehending information that was verbally presented). Their written language scores were also significantly lower than their oral expression scores. Low mathematics scores were also found, especially in solving equations and answering mathematical calculation problems. Finally, students who participated in the study had significant difficulties in the areas of problem solving and language-based critical thinking. As might be expected, this study reported that, in spite of being very verbal, persons with Asperger Syndrome had significant difficulties in understanding the oral language of others and arriving at solutions to routine problems of everyday life.

As previously suggested, children and youth with Asperger Syndrome experience difficulty in generalizing knowledge and skills. That is, they frequently have problems applying information and skills across settings and situations and with different individuals. Moreover, it is common for students with Asperger Syndrome to have difficulty attending to relevant curricular cues and stimuli.

Teachers often fail to recognize the special academic needs of students with Asperger Syndrome because these children often give the impression that they understand more than they do. That is, the deficits of some students with Asperger Syndrome are masked by their pedantic style, seemingly advanced vocabulary, and parrotlike responses, as well as by the fact that they may be good word callers without having the higher order thinking and comprehension skills to understand what they read. Some students with Asperger Syndrome may be compliant and unassertive, which contributes to this problem.

Sensory Characteristics

Both Kanner (1943) and Asperger (1944) shared the observation that children with autism and children with Asperger Syndrome are prone to peculiar sensory stimuli responses. For example, children with Asperger Syndrome are often hypersensitive to certain sounds or visual stimuli, such as fluorescent lights, and may respond negatively when overloaded with certain types of sensory stimuli. In fact, parents and teachers have reported behavior problems associated with these children's fear of anticipated stimuli such as fire alarms or chimes that are sounded at certain times. It is common for parents of children with Asperger Syndrome to report that these children have an obsessive preference for certain foods or textures (e.g., a child will wear clothes made of only certain fabrics). Some individuals with Asperger Syndrome have been reported to have an extremely high tolerance for physical pain.

Finally, many children with Asperger Syndrome engage in aberrant self-stimulatory responses such as repeatedly spinning an object for extended periods of time. In fact, the DSM–IV–TR lists "restricted repetitive and stereotyped patterns of behavior, interests, and activities" (p. 79) among the criteria for a diagnosis of Asperger Syndrome. Display of these behaviors is most common when the children experience stress, fatigue, or sensory overload (Myles, Cook, Miller, Rinner, & Robbins, 2000).

Physical and Motor Skill Anomalies

Wing (1981) observed that children with Asperger Syndrome tend to have poor motor coordination and balance problems, and these problems have been confirmed by others (Smith, 2000; Smith & Bryson, 1994). Indeed, parents and educators have found that many children and adolescents with Asperger Syndrome are awkward and clumsy, making it difficult for them to successfully participate in games involving motor skills. Because these are primary social activities for children, problems in this area have significant implications for social and pragmatic language development that go well beyond matters of motor coordination. Moreover, fine motor skill difficulties have implications for a variety of school activities, such as writing and art. Although there is some dispute over the existence of motor delays and aberrations among individuals with Asperger Syndrome (Manjiviona & Prior, 1995), there does seem to be sufficient anecdotal evidence to suggest that this is a problem that needs consideration.

Other Aspects of Asperger Syndrome

Because research in Asperger Syndrome is in its infancy, we are just beginning to understand important variables that support the intervention and treatment of children and youth with this exceptionality. The following section provides an overview of the emergent literature regarding prevalence, etiology, and comorbity of the syndrome. Also, the section discusses prognosis and outlook for individuals with Asperger Syndrome.

Prevalence

Asperger Syndrome is approximately five times more common in boys than in girls, and it has been identified throughout the world among all racial, ethnic, economic, and social groups. However, there is much debate over the number of individuals who actually have Asperger Syndrome. At the same time, its reported prevalence has increased in recent years. In large part this reported increase is a result of the addition of Asperger Syndrome to the list of pervasive developmental disorders in the DSM–IV and DSM–IV–TR and the significant attention the disorder has received in recent years.

Because of variable definitions and research methodology, current prevalence estimates for Asperger Syndrome vary considerably. For instance, Kadesjo, Gillberg, and Hagberg (1999) estimated that as many as 48 per 10,000 children could have the syndrome. In contrast, Ehlers and Gillberg (1993) estimated the prevalence to be about 36 per 10,000, and Wing (1981) speculated that the number could be as low as 1 per 10,000. Volkmar and Klin (2000) sagely noted that "the lack of a real consensus on the diagnosis of [Asperger Syndrome] means that present data are, at best, 'guestimates' of its prevalence" (p. 62). Indeed, the DSM–IV–TR lacks a prevalence estimate for Asperger Syndrome, noting that "definitive data regarding the prevalence of Asperger Syndrome are lacking" (p. 82).

Etiology

Asperger Syndrome and autism are widely considered to be the result of a neurological disorder (Autism Society of America, 1995). The Autism Society of America also strongly supports the position that there are no known psychological or environmental factors (e.g., "refrigerator mother," parental emotional aloofness, or related interpersonal variables) that cause the conditions, a position that is shared by virtually every professional and professional organization. Although the etiology of Asperger Syndrome is currently unknown, some authorities speculate that the disorder shares at least some of the same causal factors as autism (Rumsey, 1992). For example, there appears to be a significant hereditary link for cases of Asperger Syndrome (Frith, 1991). In this connection, the DSM–IV–TR notes that "there appears to be an increased frequency of Asperger's Disorder among family members of individuals who have the disorder. There may also be an increased risk for Autistic Disorder as well as more general social difficulties" (p. 82).

Comorbidity

Comorbidity refers to individuals' experiencing a greater risk of developing illnesses and related disorders, in addition to their primary disorder, than those in the general population. As with many other elements of Asperger Syndrome, the complete puzzle of whether or not individuals with this disability experience an increased vulnerability for other mental and emotional and behavioral disorders remains unsolved. Nevertheless, there are strong indications that there is a link between Asperger Syndrome and obsessive-compulsive disorder, depression, bipolar disorder, Tourette syndrome, affective disorders, attention-deficit/hyperactivity disorder, and psychosis (Volkmar & Klin, 2000).

Prognosis and Outlook

Asperger (1944) opined that most persons diagnosed with Asperger Syndrome would experience positive life outcomes based on gainful use of their special interests and unique perspectives. However, he became more guarded in this prognosis in the latter stages of his career. Currently, relatively little is known about the prognosis for persons with Asperger Syndrome. Nevertheless, there is every reason to believe that many children and youth with the syndrome will be able to lead relatively normal lives. C. L. Gillberg (1992) has voiced perhaps the most optimistic outlook, noting that "oddities of social style, communication and interests are likely to remain, but the majority of this group hold down jobs and it seems that a large proportion get married and have children" (p. 833). Others have been more guarded about the anticipated course for individuals with Asperger Syndrome (Lord & Venter, 1992; Myles, Simpson, & Becker, 1995). They have observed that the long-term prognosis for such individuals is difficult to determine due to myriad social, symptom, severity, intervention, educational, and other factors associated with the disorder. Reflecting this position, the DSM–IV–TR notes that "Asperger Disorder is a continuous and lifelong disorder" (p. 82) but that "the prognosis appears significantly better than in Autistic Disorder, as follow-up studies suggest that, as adults, many individuals are capable of gainful employment and personal self-sufficiency" (p. 82).

In spite of general agreement that the social, communication, and other characteristics associated with Asperger Syndrome comprise a devastating disability, there is also recognition that with appropriate education, treatment, and support many of these individuals can lead relatively normal and independent lives (Myles & Simpson, 2001a). Underscoring this need for appropriate treatment, Safran (2000) warned that "without appropriate educational supports, students [with Asperger Syndrome] may be left to fend for themselves in a world where social cues hold little meaning, where repeated failures in interpersonal relationships create anxiety and social rejection" (p. 154).

Case Examples

The following two case examples illustrate the major characteristics of Asperger Syndrome. Although each case is a unique example of the syndrome, both cases reflect many of the common characteristics of the disability.

 JON

Jon is an 8-year-old boy who lives with his 11-year-old sister and his mother, who is a business education teacher at a high school in their community. Jon and his sister also spend several hours each week with their father and his family.

As a baby, Jon was perceived to be happy, placid, undemanding, and not prone to cry. His parents reported that he was satisfied to lie in his crib for hours and that, although he would acknowledge their presence, he appeared to have little interest in interacting with others or being held. His parents also reported that, unlike his sister, who was assertive in seeking the attention of adults and who talked at an early age, Jon was quiet as a toddler and primarily interested in being by himself, even when around other children. Jon began speaking in single words and short sentences at around 18 months. His parents also noted that he was somewhat delayed, compared to his sister, in walking and developing self-care skills. They were advised by their physician that Jon's delays were mild and thus did not warrant an evaluation.

When Jon was 3 to 4 years old, his parents began to be very concerned about his development. They were particularly alarmed that he would wander around their house aimlessly for hours, his head tilted at an odd angle, holding his earlobes between his thumb and index finger while making a high-pitched whining noise. They also reported that he would rhythmically parrot commercials he heard on TV (which he would rarely sit and watch), including one advertisement for a detergent product, which the parents found particularly annoying. Their initial response was to ignore these behaviors, believing that their son was slow in developing and that his peculiar behaviors were satisfying some unknown need and thus should be permitted. However, at the urging of relatives, Jon's parents took him to a child psychiatrist when he was 4½. The psychiatrist diagnosed Jon as having pervasive developmental disorder–not otherwise specified and recommended that he attend a specialized preschool for at-risk and delayed children and be reevaluated annually.

At a later date, the parents reported that they did not like the psychiatrist's demeanor and thus did not seek reevaluation from him. However, they did enroll Jon in a regular preschool supported by their church. Jon attended this program until he was 6 because his parents thought he was unprepared to begin public school. Jon's preschool teachers reported that he was compliant, quiet, and placid. He passively participated in most activities and was not considered a behavior problem. He initiated few interactions with peers, although he would respond to peer initiations. At the age of 6, Jon was enrolled in kindergarten at his neighborhood school. Shortly afterward, the parents separated, and they were divorced approximately a year later. The parents reported that the period of separation and divorce was very difficult for their daughter but that Jon appeared to be oblivious to his father's absence.

Jon currently attends a regular second-grade classroom at a neighborhood elementary school. He is eligible for itinerant special education services (his teacher regularly meets with a special education teacher to discuss curriculum adaptations for Jon) and receives weekly 1-hour individualized speech–language services; however, his teacher describes him as an "average" student. His teacher reports that Jon is slow to complete assignments and often appears confused regarding classroom expectations. However, she notes that once he "catches on" to a task, he will obsessively work to complete it. She also notes that he is generally compliant and appears vaguely interested in pleasing her. She also observes that he is extremely orderly in arranging books and other materials in his desk and sometimes appears overwrought when classroom schedule changes occur. For example, a recent rainstorm required that the children complete their recess in the classroom, a change that appeared to be very hard for Jon to comprehend.

Jon typically stands next to his teacher on the playground, except when he occasionally obsessively wanders the perimeter of the school grounds. Jon is shy and socially isolated from his peers. He will respond briefly when approached by peers; however, he has yet to be observed initiating contact or joining in any games. Jon tends to be very passive, and on more than one occasion he has been bullied by other boys at recess. On these occasions Jon retreats from the aggressor and stands by his teacher.

Jon's mother reports that his behavior of wandering with his head tilted at an odd angle while holding his earlobes and making high-pitched whining noises has decreased significantly over the past year. However, he sometimes obsessively rubs and flaps his hands when he is agitated or stressed.

Approximately a year ago Jon was evaluated at a university child guidance clinic. The mother and father were somewhat disturbed by the diagnosis of Asperger Syndrome. However, after learning more about the condition, they seemed to be willing to accept their son's disability. They seem committed to supporting his continued development.

TERRY

Terry is 17 and lives with his mother, father, and younger brother. An older sister attends a nearby state university and lives with the family during the summers. The family is middle class, with both parents holding engineering positions.

Terry was only recently diagnosed with Asperger Syndrome by a multidisciplinary evaluation team at a children's hospital. Prior to receiving that diagnosis, Terry had been identified as being learning disabled, "mildly autistic," and schizophrenic and as having attention-deficit/hyperactivity disorder and a developmental expressive language disorder.

Early records reveal that Terry was slightly delayed in starting to walk and in developing expressive language. He spoke using one or two words until about age 3, at which time he almost overnight began speaking in long and complicated sentences. Terry's speech is currently quite pedantic, and other students at his school sometimes call him "professor." However, his conversations are limited to a few set topics, and his overall communication demeanor is marked by an absence of affect and inflection.

Since he was a young child, Terry has maintained an obsessive interest in toilets and related plumbing equipment. His parents reported that when he was as young as 5 he knew the brand name of the toilets in his home, day-care center, father's and mother's businesses, and several of the stores in a nearby shopping center. He also displayed a number of stereotyped repetitive behaviors until he was about 10, including spinning empty 1-liter cola containers and tilting his head and squinting at persons by whom he was standing. He no longer spins cola containers; however, he continues to stare and squint at others with his head tilted.

Terry's family and schoolmates have described him as "odd" since the time he began school. He has never been able to mix with peers, although he daily watches his classmates talk in the hallways between classes. He has occasionally approached classmates; however, his limited repertoire of interests, such as his tendency to describe the plumbing fixtures in the school, has alienated him from his classmates.

According to his parents and teachers, Terry has never had a true friend. In spite of his mother's repeated attempts to arrange relationships with age peers through neighbors and friends and his teachers' development of peer support programs, Terry has remained a loner. Recently, Terry began a program in his special education resource room (where he spends 2 hours daily working on study and social skills) in which general education students participate in social activities with special education students. In this program Terry is routinely the one with whom the students least want to interact, even though the other special education students have fewer cognitive, language, and academic abilities and skills. When one general education classmate was queried about this circumstance, she responded, "He is such a geek—he gets right in my face and only wants to talk about the sinks in the boys' bathroom."

When asked about his future, Terry responds that he wants to be a plumber (an interest his teachers have recently attempted to cultivate to harness his obsessive interest in plumbing fixtures). He also indicates that he wants to marry and be a member of the community Lion's Club. His parents and siblings worry about Terry's future after he completes school, fearing that he will be unprepared to work or live outside the home.

Concluding Thoughts

There is considerable debate regarding whether Asperger Syndrome is an element of the so-called autism spectrum or an independent disability unconnected to autism. In spite of this spirited debate, professionals agree that the syndrome is a serious social and communication disorder that can have devastating effects. However, there is also agreement that the general prognosis for individuals with Asperger Syndrome is relatively good and that with support and training these individuals can be productive citizens.

Assessing Students with Asperger Syndrome

2

Authored with Judith K. Carlson

Prescriptive diagnostic assessment of students with Asperger Syndrome involves collecting data with the specific purpose of verifying student strengths and concerns. Such data may include a medical history, intelligence and aptitude ratings, academic test scores, and anecdotal records of the student's daily life. Regardless of the source of this data, assessment should focus on academic, behavioral, social, physical, and environmental components (Klin, Sparrow, Marans, Carter, & Volkmar, 2000; Myles & Adreon, 2001; Myles, Constant, Simpson, & Carlson, 1989; Szatmari, 1991). This information is collected to provide the student with appropriate educational placement, to target goals and objectives, to monitor student progress, and to evaluate the quality of the educational services being received. In addition, multidisciplinary teams may be created to assess across areas such as occupational and physical therapy, audiology, vision, sensory motor therapy, and social work.

Norm-Referenced Assessment

In norm-referenced assessment, standardized tests are used to collect data. Generally, norm-referenced tests use specified questions and administration and scoring procedures. The assumption underlying norm-referenced assessment is that every student receives the same questions and the same administration. The test taker's performance is compared to the performance of the norm group; a norm group consists of randomly selected students who share certain characteristics.

Items on a norm-referenced test are carefully compiled according to the results of earlier tests conducted with students in the norm group. At the same time, scores on the norm-referenced test are statistically determined by the distribution of scores from the norm group.

Administration of a norm-referenced test is usually specified in detail. If the examiner violates the required administration procedures, the scores obtained in that testing are not valid. Because a norm-referenced test compares the test taker's performance to that of the norm group, it is necessary to conduct the test in the same way as the norm group experienced it.

Usually, a norm-referenced test yields two or more kinds of scores. First, the student's performance is calculated as a raw score. Next, the raw score is converted to a standard score for comparison with the performance of the norm group. Because the norm group represents the general population from a statistical viewpoint, an examiner can compare a student's performance with that of similar students in the nation.

Norm-Referenced Measures Appropriate for Students with Asperger Syndrome

Many of the more popular norm-referenced tests were created with norm samples that did not contain students with Asperger Syndrome. Thus, examiners must use extra caution when administering and interpreting results of such tests with this population. An examiner should consult the test manual to determine whether the test's norm group is appropriate for the student being assessed. Commonly used norm-referenced tests for students with exceptionalities, including those with Asperger Syndrome, are (a) diagnostic measures, (b) aptitude and achievement tests, (c) tests of adaptive behavior and social skills, (d) sensory measures, and (e) speech–language assessment.

Diagnostic Measures

Because Asperger Syndrome is a medical diagnosis, physicians typically provide to parents and educators the official documentation that a child or youth has the syndrome. It is difficult, however, for medical professionals to quickly and accurately determine whether a child or youth has Asperger Syndrome, because brief observations are most often not sufficient to render a diagnosis. Thus, the psychiatrists and other physicians must rely, in great part, on the observations and reports of parents and teachers who know the individual well.

To date, two norm-referenced measures, the *Asperger Syndrome Diagnostic Scale* (ASDS; Myles, Bock, & Simpson, 2000) and the *Gilliam Asperger Disorder Scale* (GADS; Gilliam, 2001), exist that can assist medical, mental health, and educational professionals in determining whether a child or youth has Asperger Syndrome. The ASDS is a 50-item measure that was normed on 227 individuals with Asperger Syndrome, attention-deficit/hyperactivity disorder, autism, learning disabilities, and behavioral disorders. The ASDS can be completed in 10 to 15 minutes by any adult who knows well the person being diagnosed. The ASDS has five subscales: (a) language, (b) social, (c) maladaptions, (d) cognition, and (e) sensory-motor. Respondents indicate the presence or absence of characteristics in each of these areas; the resulting standard score indicates the probability that the child or youth has Asperger Syndrome and differentiates it from attention-deficit/hyperactivity disorder, autism, learning disabilities, and behavioral disorders. Parents or teachers can complete the ASDS and present it to the diagnostic professional, who can then use it as an aid in rendering a correct diagnosis.

The GADS, normed on 107 individuals, is designed to distinguish children and youth ages 3 to 22 who have Asperger Syndrome from those with autism and other behavioral disorders. It contains 32 items that describe specific, observable, and measurable behaviors that are divided into four subscales. Designed to be completed by parents and professionals, this instrument provides standard scores and percentile ranks to determine the likelihood that an individual has Asperger Syndrome. Completion time for the GADS is approximately 5 to 10 minutes.

Aptitude and Achievement Tests

All general intelligence tests can be used with students with Asperger Syndrome. There are advantages and disadvantages of using such tests, depending on the skills and capabilities of the individual student and the examiner. The *Wechsler Intelligence Scale for Children–Third Edition* (WISC–III; Wechsler, 1991) and the *Stanford–Binet Intelligence Scale–Fourth Edition* (Thorndike, Hagen, & Sattler, 1985) are widely used intelligence tests in the fields of education and psychology. Standardized scores yielded by most other norm-referenced tests are comparable with scores of these two intelligence tests.

It is important to note that no students with Asperger Syndrome were identified in the norm groups for these two tests. It is possible to substitute other standardized measures that may more directly assess the abilities of students with Asperger Syndrome.

Tests of Adaptive Behavior and Social Skills

Behaviorial and social skills are common deficits for students with Asperger Syndrome (American Psychiatric Association, 2000; Wing, 1991; World Health Organization, 1992). Thus, it is important to assess these areas thoroughly.

The *Behavior Assessment System for Children* (BASC; Reynolds & Kamphaus, 1992) assesses emotional and behavioral issues in children and youth with Asperger Syndrome, as well as other special needs. This instrument, which contains a Parent Rating Scale, Teacher Rating Scale, and Student Self-Report, examines a variety of areas, including (a) hyperactivity, (b) conduct problems, (c) aggression, (d) anxiety, (e) depression, (f) withdrawal, (g) attention problems, (h) adaptability, (i) leadership, and (j) social skills. The BASC has been used to identify areas of concern and to aid in designing treatment plans for students with Asperger Syndrome (Barnhill, Hagiwara, Myles, Simpson, et al., 2000).

The *Vineland Adaptive Behavior Scales* (VABS; Sparrow, Balla, & Cicchetti, 1984) is frequently used to examine behavioral and social skills of children with Asperger Syndrome. There are three independent forms of the VABS. Two of the forms, the Expanded Form and the Survey Form, are administered by interviewing the student's primary caregiver. The third form is the Classroom Edition, which is conducted with a teacher. All three forms assess the domains of communication, daily living, socialization, and motor skills. The Expanded Form and the Survey Form also assess a maladaptive behavior domain.

Sensory Measures

Many children and youth manifest sensory issues in each of the seven sensory areas: (a) tactile, (b) vestibular, (c) proprioception, (d) visual, (e) auditory, (f) gustatory, and (g) olfactory (Dunn, Myles, & Orr, 2002; Rinner, 2000). Thus, it is important that these areas be part of a comprehensive assessment. Three sensory measures exist that can compare the sensory profile of children and youth with Asperger Syndrome to neurotypical individuals: (a) the *Sensory Profile* (Dunn, 1999), (b) the *Short Sensory Profile* (McIntosh, Miller, Shyu, & Dunn, 1999), and (c) the *Sensory Integration and Praxis Test* (SIPT; Ayres, 1989) (Myles, Cook, Miller, Rinner, & Robbins, 2000). One instrument, the *Sensory Profile*, not only assesses sensory issues but also looks at the impact of sensory problems on emotional and behavioral issues.

Speech–Language Assessment

Language assessments that go beyond word pronunciation, vocabulary, sentence structure, and grammar are needed to understand the language issues of children and youth with Asperger Syndrome (Bligh, cited in Michael Thompson Productions, 2000; Myles & Adreon, 2001). Specifically, speech–language assessment should include pragmatics, the social part of language; understanding of nonliteral language; verbal problem solving; and nonverbal communication. Bligh recommended the following norm-referenced instruments as helpful in program planning:

- *Clinical Evaluation of Language Fundamentals–Third Edition* (Semel, Wiig, & Secord, 1995)

- *Comprehensive Receptive and Expressive Vocabulary Test* (Wallace & Hammill, 1994)

- *Test of Language Competence–Expanded Edition* (Wiig & Secord, 1989)

- *Test of Pragmatic Language* (Phelps-Terasaki & Phelps-Gunn, 1992)

- *Test of Problem Solving–Elementary, Revised* (Zachman, Huisingh, Barrett, Orman, & LoGiudice, 1994)

- *Test of Problem Solving–Adolescent* (Zachman, Barrett, Huisingh, Orman, & Blagden, 1991).

Informal Assessment

Informal assessment refers to a practitioner's collecting, evaluating, and applying information about a student. The data obtained through informal assessment are frequently used to set goals, identify instructional strategies, and measure outcome behaviors (Guerin & Maier, 1983). Informal assessment procedures target what the student knows and how the student learns, allowing practitioners to select instructional techniques that facilitate learning.

Informal assessment does not require a reference group against which to measure student performance. Rather, students are compared to their own performance levels within the curriculum and the demands of the program or placement. Therefore, data can be collected in a variety of settings: classroom, home, workplace, clinic, and testing facility. Information obtained through informal assessment frequently involves ordinary classroom interactions (Guerin & Maier, 1983; Klin, Sparrow, et al., 2000).

The physical environment, task presentation, level of interest, and past learning experience can all influence how well a person with Asperger Syndrome performs on a test. Informal assessment requires no rigid time constraints or standardized procedures. As a result, students with Asperger Syndrome can approach problem solving in traditional or nontraditional ways. Because no time limit is specified, the examiner can start and progress as he or she becomes familiar with the student, allowing time to build rapport (Myles, Bock, & Simpson, 2000).

Designing an assessment to elicit certain behaviors can also provide important information. For example, is the student able to ask for help or indicate that he or she would like to take a break from the test? If not, how does the student communicate needs? Understanding a student's functioning level can lead to an understanding of how the student approaches tasks and indicates readiness skills in academics or social development. This information can aid in establishing realistic goals that are crucial for encouraging learning and building success. Setting multiple goals—those that the student can readily accomplish, those that are more difficult, and those that are challenging, yet motivating—helps to create a best-practices intervention program. Throughout testing, the examiner should identify which tasks are easy or difficult for the student and note which activities, materials, and methods receive the most positive response.

Although it can be used as part of a full evaluation battery, informal assessment is best suited for data collection that is ongoing and fluid. Revising Individualized Education Program objectives, selecting instruction and response formats, modifying assignments, setting time frames for performance, and developing individualized curricula can all be enhanced by use of informal assessment data.

Areas of Consideration

Myles et al. (1989) listed major areas of consideration for using informal assessment with students with Asperger Syndrome. These areas include (a) stimulus overselectivity, (b) motivation, and (c) self-stimulatory behaviors.

Stimulus Overselectivity

Stimulus overselectivity occurs when a student eliminates all but a few cues in the environment. For example, when shown word cards with the verbal instruction "Point to the card with the word *exit* on it," the student may continually select the card on the left. This response pattern can be disrupted by varying the presentation of the task, the arrangement of the stimuli, or the manner in which the examiner requests the information.

Motivation

Limited motivation can be confused with inability to complete a task or lack of interest in the task. Students with Asperger Syndrome frequently require external motivation to complete a task. Prior to testing, it is important to determine appropriate reinforcers, break times, and preferred tasks. Talking with parents, teachers, caregivers, and the student can provide several reinforcers to mitigate limited motivation. Such reinforcers as tangible objects, picture boards, or simple tokens can motivate the student to complete the task.

Self-Stimulatory Behaviors

Some students with Asperger Syndrome exhibit self-stimulatory behaviors such as spinning objects. If these repetitive movements are not interfering with test administration or response, they should be ignored during the assessment. If the self-stimulatory behaviors are disruptive, however, it may be necessary to work with the student to achieve appropriate response behaviors. Regardless, anecdotal records regarding the student's self-stimulatory behaviors should be maintained because they can provide valuable information about the student's frustration levels and coping mechanisms.

Academic Areas

Evaluation of the student with Asperger Syndrome must include the three major academic areas: reading, mathematics, and oral and written language. An assessment that encompasses these areas will provide foundation information for use in instruction.

Assessment of each of these areas can involve use of commercial tests, a "scope-and-sequence" approach, or the school's own curriculum. Commercial items are beneficial because they usually take little time to prepare and often apply to a wide range of skills. Examples of commercial tests are the *Hudson Educational Skills Inventory* (HESI; Hudson, Colson, & Welch, 1989) and the *Brigance Diagnostic Inventory of Essential Skills* (Brigance, 1980).

With a scope-and-sequence approach, a skill or concept is broken down into its component parts. The first component is taught and practiced until it is mastered. Then the next component is taught, and so on. A scope and sequence can be developed for most academic, functional, behavioral, social, and vocational areas. A scope-and-sequence approach is invaluable for students with Asperger Syndrome, especially when they have splinter skills. A student has a splinter skill if he or she can complete a specific step of a task, yet not be able to complete prior or subsequent steps. For example, a student may be able to recite the numbers 1 through 200, yet not be able to understand the concept of one-to-one correspondence. Looking at a math scope and sequence will show where rote counting falls on a continuum of math skills and what skills lie between understanding the concept of one-to-one correspondence and counting numbers up to 200. Consideration should be given to the individual student's learning preferences when selecting a scope-and-sequence approach for assessment or intervention. Students who favor a simultaneous or "big picture" approach do not perform well with a scope-and-sequence approach.

Curriculum-based assessments are advantageous for most students because items are drawn from the school's curriculum. Students are assessed on skills that are taught in school, in the order that they are presented. The major disadvantage of this type of assessment is the time that it takes to develop an assessment protocol. A secondary disadvantage is the focus of the assessment. That is, emphasis is typically placed on whether or not the student can perform a task, not on how the student approaches the task. The latter, of course, has great instructional implications. As with the scope-and-sequence approach, in curriculum-based assessments, splinter skills and student learning preferences must be considered.

Reading

Reading is a complex area to assess because many of the sub-skills are interrelated. For students with Asperger Syndrome, the major consideration should be comprehension. Although many students with the syndrome may exhibit solid mechanical reading skills (i.e., appropriate decoding and sight word skills), their understanding of passages and their ability to relate that understanding to everyday experience may be limited. As students progress through the educational system, mechanical abilities become less important, and understanding and generalization become more critical. Thus, reading assessment of children and youth with Asperger Syndrome must emphasize comprehension and application (Sundbye, 2001; Sundbye & McCoy, 1997).

A composite of specialized subareas must be developed, resulting in an individualized and integrated reading assessment plan for each student. Two basic reading levels must be established. First is the student's independent reading level, that level at which the student can read with 98% to 100% word accuracy and demonstrate comprehension of 90% to 100%. Second is the student's instructional reading level, that level at which the student can recognize words with 95% accuracy and demonstrate comprehension of 75% or higher. These data must be determined both orally and silently (Sundbye, 2001).

This information can be gained through a curriculum-based assessment or through a commercial informal reading inventory, such as the *Classroom Reading Inventory* (Silvaroli, 1986) or the *Durrell Analysis of Reading Difficulty* (Durrell & Catterson, 1981).

It is important to select comprehension questions that will evaluate both recognition and recall response levels (Hudson, Colson, & Braxdale, 1984). Students with Asperger Syndrome may be able to answer general information questions only understanding the information on a basic level; hence, it is necessary to develop questions that address a variety of comprehension levels. In addition to factual and vocabulary questions (part of most commercial informal reading inventories), inferential and main idea questions must also be included, along with assessment of the ability to predict outcome, draw conclusions, and distinguish fact from fantasy (Sundbye, 2001).

The ability to sequence visual materials is a necessary prerequisite for more complex comprehension; consequently, any student who has difficulty with passage comprehension should be assessed in this area. This ability can be assessed with a series of three or more picture cards (the more cards, the more complex the process) that describe the steps of an activity. Commercial sequencing cards can be used; however, if a student has difficulty responding to such materials, the examiner can make an informal series of cards based on a common activity that is familiar to the student (e.g., brushing teeth).

A miscue analysis should be performed on oral reading passages at the student's instructional level. This involves examining the pattern of errors in the passages, emphasizing such qualities as the incorrect word's graphic similarity to the printed word, the occurrence of interclass (e.g., noun for verb) and intraclass (e.g., noun for noun) substitutions, and percentage of self-corrections. Such analysis supplements the traditional error marking recommended in many informal reading inventories (i.e., those focusing on differentiating substitutions, omissions, deletions, and repetitions). Miscue analysis may give insight into the student's reading skills as a total process, including use of context, logic cues, word recognition, and analysis (Stanford & Siders, 2001).

The student's listening capacity should also be assessed. This is the level at which students comprehend material read aloud. The examiner reads passages, starting one grade level above a student's established instructional reading level and continuing until a student demonstrates less than 75% comprehension. Although it is common for normally achieving learners to exhibit a higher capacity for listening than for oral or silent reading, this may not be the case for the student with Asperger Syndrome (Sundbye, 2001).

The student's contextual analysis strengths and weaknesses may be determined by using a cloze procedure. This involves taking a reading passage of approximately 250 words at the student's instructional level and systematically deleting every seventh or ninth word. The first and last sentences of the passage remain intact. The student then silently reads the passage, filling in the blanks based on the context. Intraclass substitutions that make sense in context should be accepted as correct. Analysis focuses on the types of cues (e.g., surrounding words, pictures, bold or italic print, or the general story plot) used to interpret the material (Sundbye, 2001).

The student's response to certain teaching techniques, such as language experience approach or morphographic or multisensory reading, can also be examined as a part of the assessment process. For example, to analyze the effectiveness of the language experience approach, the student creates and dictates a story to the examiner. Different stimuli such as pictures, open-ended sentences, and activities can be used for story development. The examiner then selects words from the story, writes them on flash cards, and practices with the student. Finally, the complete story is read, first in a choral format (examiner and student reading aloud simultaneously) and then independently by the student. The examiner compares the student's reading abilities using the self-generated stories and published reading materials.

With comprehension as the major assessment focus for students with Asperger Syndrome, the remaining areas in a traditional reading assessment battery (word analysis and word recognition) may carry little importance, because it is possible that students with Asperger Syndrome may have adequate analysis and recognition skills. However, when additional information is desired, further assessment may be used.

A phonics measure can be used to determine specific phonetic components students use in word analysis (decoding). Most commercial phonics measures are based on the formation of nonsense words, thus isolating consonants, vowels, blends, digraphs, and diphthongs. Two factors must be considered when determining the need to administer a phonics measure. First, for students in mainstream educational settings, phonics training traditionally ends during the early elementary years. Accordingly, phonics instruction is usually recommended only in cases where a student has already acquired and demonstrated the majority of basic phonics skills, thus allowing for training in specific skill areas. The second factor relates to the application of phonetic skills in reading. Some students may exhibit an overreliance on phonics, without regard to non–rule-based pronunciations or contextual clues (Sundbye, 2001).

Word recognition is assessed by determining the student's sight word vocabulary. This may take several directions, depending on the student's age and reading skills. Core word lists such as those by Dolch (1955) or Fry (1980) can be used to identify words students should know by sight by grade level. These lists are particularly useful with younger students who have limited reading vocabularies or who are in inclusive environments. For older students who exhibit limited vocabulary, sight word lists stressing survival words (e.g., Brigance, 1980) should be included in the assessment package. Table 2.1 provides an overview of the diagnostic sequence in reading.

Mathematics

Mathematics is typically considered a hierarchical subject. That is, if early skills are not established, further skills cannot be mastered. Each skill is thought of in terms of components because many mathematic skills include a number of components.

This traditional understanding of mathematics knowledge and skill acquisition applies to the student with Asperger Syndrome. The student with Asperger Syndrome may have computation skills without having prerequisite readiness skills. For example, the student with splinter skills (e.g., computation skills in the absence of numerical understanding) has not mastered a meaningful task. Instead, the student has memorized a rote skill, which serves little functional purpose. The skill holds no meaning for the student; it cannot be applied to any simulated or

Table 2.1
Diagnostic Sequence in Reading

Sequence for Older Elementary Children

    A. Informal reading inventory (silent and oral)
        1. Curriculum-based
        2. Commercial
    B. Miscue analysis
    C. Levels of comprehension (recognition and recall)
        1. Factual
        2. Inferential
        3. Main idea
        4. Predicting outcomes
        5. Drawing conclusions
        6. Fact versus fantasy
        7. Vocabulary
        8. Sequencing
    D. Listening capacity
    E. Cloze procedures
    F. Fluency and rate

Sequence for Younger Elementary Children

    A. Informal reading inventory (silent and oral)
        1. Curriculum-based
        2. Commercial
    B. Miscue analysis
    C. Levels of comprehension (recognition and recall)
        1. Factual
        2. Inferential
        3. Main idea
        4. Predicting outcomes
        5. Drawing conclusions
        6. Fact versus fantasy
        7. Vocabulary
        8. Sequencing
    D. Listening capacity
    E. Phonics (in isolation and within words)

(continues)

Table 2.1

Diagnostic Sequence in Reading *Continued.*

Sequence for Younger Elementary Children *Continued.*

    F. Sight words (flash and analysis)

    G. Alphabet recognition (particulary if low phonics or sight words)

    H. Language experience

       1. Reads own written stories

       2. Reads own words on flash cards

       3. Comprehends own stories (recognition and recall)

    I. Sequencing of visual material and relating story

---

real-life setting. Thus, mathematics must be considered a hierarchical subject for students with Asperger Syndrome, and assessment of this area must proceed sequentially. Specific attention should be paid to basic concepts, computation, problem solving, and functional skills.

Basic concepts assessment determines whether students with Asperger Syndrome have mastered skills basic to the understanding of mathematics. According to Piaget (1959) and Mercer (1996), these skills include the following:

- Classification—the ability to judge similarities and differences by color, shape, size, or function

- Number conservation—the ability to deduce that amounts remain the same even when appearances change (e.g., the amount of water in two different containers is equal)

- Ordering and seriation—the ability to arrange items without considering the quantitative relationship between them or to arrange items based on a change in a property (e.g., arranging items of various lengths from shortest to longest)

- One-to-one correspondence—the ability to understand that one object in a set is the same number as one object in another set, regardless of characteristics (e.g., six apples represent the same quantity as six buttons)

These skills should be assessed systematically at the concrete, semiconcrete, and abstract levels.

Computation involves the calculation of an equation. This basic mathematics area may be a strength for students with Asperger Syndrome. That is, these students may be able to answer problems correctly without understanding the process underlying the calculation. A test that probes comprehension of the proper algorithm, or computational method, is the *Clinical Math Interview* (CMI; Skrtic, Kvam, & Beals, 1983). After working designated problems, a student with Asperger Syndrome explains in an interview format how problems were solved. CMI administration reveals (a) a student's current level of arithmetic functioning, (b) how a student works a problem, and (c) whether a student is dependent on incorrect algorithms. Analysis of computation errors can reveal information about a student's mathematical skills in four categories (Roberts, 1968):

- Wrong operation—the student performs an operation other than the one that is required to solve the problem

- Computational error—the student applies the correct operation, but the response is based on errors in recalling number facts

- Defective algorithm—the student applies the correct operation but makes errors other than fact

- Random response—the student's response shows no discernible relationship to the problem

Problem solving is the ability to use computational skills meaningfully to solve word or story problems. According to Reisman (1972), a problem is used to initiate this type of learning. Problem solving is dependent on knowledge and application of basic concepts, computation, and generalization. Problem-solving assessment must consider a student's ability to (a) identify important features in a problem-solving situation, (b) translate a verbal sentence into a mathematical sentence, and (c) calculate a solution (Shure, 1992). Assessment must reveal a student's competence at each level of problem solving. Students with Asperger Syndrome typically demonstrate difficulty with nonrote skills, such as identifying important problem-solving features and translating a verbal sentence into a mathematical sentence.

Functional skills assessment involves the use of computational and problem-solving skills to respond to real-life situations. Functional skills include calculations involving time, money, measurement, and geometry. These are particularly important to students with Asperger Syndrome because they are potential life skills. In fact, the goal of instruction in the other mathematical areas (i.e., basic skills, computation, problem solving) should be to assist students with Asperger Syndrome in successfully using functional skills. Thus, assessment of these skills is extremely important. Table 2.2 provides an overview of the diagnostic sequence in mathematics.

Oral and Written Language

Because students with Asperger Syndrome often have a variety of unique language characteristics (e.g., perseveration, idiosyncratic language), assessment of oral and written language may present particular problems. Unfortunately, oral language is not an area most educators are trained to address; therefore, they tend to refer children with problems in this area to a speech–language pathologist (Harn, Bradsaw, & Ogletree, 1999; Moran, 1982). Such a diagnostic referral may be helpful, but it usually does not address all pertinent classroom-related skills, activities, and issues. Although language acquisition follows a developmental sequence, it is not as clearly hierarchical as math and thus requires a different assessment approach. Because the ability to communicate is partially dependent on the environment, it is necessary to examine a student's language in a variety of settings and conditions to form an adequate picture of his or her language skills and to determine appropriate areas for intervention (Harn et al., 1999).

Normally developing and achieving students provide teachers with numerous spontaneous language samples that allow for assessment in natural settings. They tell stories, converse on the playground, and engage in role playing. These samples can be tape-recorded for subsequent transcription and analysis. To produce stories or conversations for analysis, students with Asperger Syndrome, on the other hand, may need additional encouragement, stimulus, or preplanning. For example, a special

Table 2.2
Diagnostic Sequence in Mathematics

Sequence for Older Elementary Children

A. Overview of skills
   1. Number/notation
   2. Mathematical language
   3. Ordinality
   4. Place value
   5. Geometric concepts
   6. Fractions
   7. Measurement
   8. Mathematical applications
   9. Word problems
   10. Estimation
   11. Graphing

B. Probes based on difficulties with overview skills

C. Informal math inventory

D. Error pattern analysis

E. Clinical Math Interview (CMI)

Sequence for Younger Elementary Children

A. Overview of skills based on Piaget's levels (concrete, semiconcrete, abstract)
   1. Numeration
   2. Mathematical language
   3. Measurement
   4. Place value
   5. One-to-one correspondence
   6. Geometry
   7. Computation
   8. Fractions
   9. Conservation of sets
   10. Graphing

B. Probes based on difficulties with overview skills

C. Word problems presented orally

D. Math facts presentation (flash and analysis)

occasion, such as a field trip or a movie, may be used as a topic of discussion. Also, with some students with Asperger Syndrome, a picture or topic may be used to produce a sample.

Written language samples can be elicited in much the same way, that is, by asking a student to tell a story in writing, with or without prompts. However, examiners must keep in mind the motor skills of a student with Asperger Syndrome. If the student has motor problems, two written samples may be gathered: one written by hand and one generated on a computer.

Oral and written language samples can be analyzed and compared on a number of variables. Because oral language generally precedes written language, it is reasonable to expect that most students' oral samples will be more complex than their written work. Thus, oral abilities are most often analyzed to determine initial instructional priorities and to group students for language instruction. If teachers wish to compare a student's language development to that of his or her peers, parallel samples may be taken from an average student of the same age and gender. Many of the elements considered in language assessment are subjective; therefore, care should be taken to consider language samples in the context of both the current environment and the child's cultural background. Language differences due to ethnic background should not be confused with language problems; these have different instructional implications (Johnson, 1996).

An initial area of language assessment is communicative content, which focuses on answering the following questions: What type of story did the student relate? Did it have a beginning, middle, and end? Was it coherent? Was it interesting and creative?

Complexity of language should also be considered. Such assessment examines the proportion of simple, compound, and complex sentences. In written language, this analysis focuses on what a student intended rather than on punctuation, for instance, Does the student use only one sentence type or demonstrate ability to use a variety of simple and complex forms? Is there a difference between oral and written sentence length and complexity? Does the student use an effective descriptive vocabulary? Does the student use colorful adjectives and phrases or choose simple words that can be correctly applied and spelled with confidence? Does the student possess a vocabulary adequate to communicate his or her intent?

Grammar is a third area for language analysis and comparison. It includes most of the features of language generally taught in English classes, including subject–verb agreement, pronoun usage, correct usage of word endings to indicate verb tense, plurals, and possessives. As in other areas of assessment, an effort should be made to distinguish between environmental or cultural differences in language and the student's lack of a specific language skill.

Transcription skills are an additional written language consideration. Specifically, this includes appropriate use of capital letters, punctuation, spelling, and handwriting. Spelling errors are analyzed as to type, that is, whether misspelling of words is rule based (i.e., caused by overreliance on rules, such as "*i* before *e* except after *c*"), predictable, or unpredictable.

Additional issues related to understanding language in context may need to be examined in students with language-related learning problems. Some students with Asperger Syndrome are extremely literal and inflexible, acknowledging only one meaning for a word. Others have not developed a schema or framework that enables them to relate new words to words already in their vocabulary. A simple way to assess these problems is to devise activities that assess knowledge of common idioms or proverbs (e.g., ask the student to explain "Don't cry over spilt milk") or that check understanding of categorical grouping (e.g., "How do these things go together—fork, knife, and spoon?"). Understanding of synonyms and antonyms may be assessed in a similar manner.

A final language area to examine is the student's knowledge of school vocabulary, that is, those words that frequently appear in oral and written directions or that are necessary to understand particular subject matter (e.g., in math, *calculate, solve, determine*). If a student cannot understand the vocabulary used to convey instructions or deliver content, appropriate responses cannot be expected. Table 2.3 provides an overview of the diagnostic sequence in oral and written language.

Student Learning Traits

A student's achievement is influenced by a variety of factors. External factors, such as the bus ride to school or where the student's desk is located in the classroom, have an impact that is often easy to recognize and observe. Internal factors, such as how students

Table 2.3
Diagnostic Sequence in Oral and Written Language

Sequence for Older Elementary Children

A. Oral language sample (with and without brainstorming)

B. Written language sample (with and without brainstorming)

C. Spelling of known words (looking for organization)
  1. Rule based
  2. Predictable and unpredictable words
  3. Retest words missed in writing in oral mode
  4. Retest words missed at recall level using recognition level
  5. Retest words missed at recognition level using proofing format

D. Capitalization and punctuation (in contrived sample)

E. Following multistep directions (in written and oral modes)

F. Idioms, synonyms, antonyms, categories

G. Academic language in content areas

H. Near/far point copying

Sequence for Younger Elementary Children

A. Oral language sample (with different stimuli)

B. Language experience story

C. Sequencing

D. Written language sample (one sentence from story or story creation)

E. Writing alphabet (from memory or from model if reversals appear)

F. Personal information (name, address, telephone number)

G. Spelling of known words
  1. Retest words missed in writing in oral mode
  2. Retest words missed at recall level using recognition level
  3. Retest words missed at recognition level using proofing format

H. Following multistep directions (in written and oral modes)

I. Idioms, synonyms, antonyms, categories

J. Academic language in content areas

K. Near/far point copying

perceive or receive information, how they process and store concepts, and how they apply these data to their daily lives are more elusive; however, this type of variable must be measured subjectively, through direct observation of the student, examination of classroom materials and setting demands, and pinpointing of instructional and response preferences. These indicators of how children learn are called student learning traits.

According to Myles et al. (1989), student learning traits offer insight into how students with Asperger Syndrome gain information across academic areas. For example, a student may respond to only meaningful stimuli and not to rote stimuli. Some students may be sequential learners, preferring tasks presented in a part-to-whole format, whereas others may favor a simultaneous, "big picture" approach. There are as many learning traits as there are students, and each student possesses specific traits. Student learning traits have been divided into three basic categories: learning and memory, behavioral patterns and characteristics, and strategies.

Learning and Memory

Learning and memory refer to those skills that allow students to focus their attention and store information. Sequential versus simultaneous processing, stimulus selectivity, and attention to detail are all in this category. A student's memory skills, including short-term, long-term, visual, auditory, rote, and meaningful memory, play a role in creating the individual's learning style. Tasks that examine students' preferences and strengths within these areas can be contrived and observed for the purpose of shaping instruction.

A student's rate of performance and task pacing also contribute to learning style. Take, for example, the case of Trudy, a young woman with Asperger Syndrome who was being served in a residential treatment center for adolescents with severe behavioral problems. Trudy was thought to be stubborn and oppositional by her house staff, teachers, and therapists because she rarely answered questions or offered input during school and therapy sessions. An examination of Trudy's learning style revealed that she needed a wait time of 20 to 30 seconds to access and process information, rather than the traditional 3- to

5-second wait time experienced in reciprocal conversation. When given adequate wait time, Trudy was able to offer insights and actively participate in her program goals. Incidental learning, independent work habits, and generalization skills round out this category of student learning traits.

Behavioral Patterns and Characteristics

How students act on environmental stimuli and retrieved information and the unique way they apply this information to daily functioning reveal their behavioral patterns and characteristics. All types of interactional patterns are observed, including adult-to-student, student-to-peer, and small- and large-group interchanges. The student's pattern of response to reinforcement, structure, stress, and success should also be examined. Further, avoidance behaviors, attention-seeking behaviors, and self-stimulatory patterns are all part of a student's behavioral profile. Through structured observation of the student in a variety of settings, the examiner can note on-task and off-task characteristics, flexibility in moving from one activity to the next, and the type of events that trigger impulsive or compulsive behavior.

For students with Asperger Syndrome, some specific behavioral patterns must be considered. The use of echolalia as a communication tool, the ability to make and maintain eye contact, and the level of distractibility and perseverance are all important links to successful classroom performance. Eye, hand, and foot dominance, as well as the ability to cross midline, must also be examined to determine perceptual abilities and fine- and gross-motor skills. These areas can easily be tapped by having the student visually track a favorite toy, catch and kick a ball, and draw or write. Midline issues can be addressed by having the student complete a simple shape or interlocking puzzle. The examiner places puzzle pieces on opposite sides of the puzzle board and observes whether the student reaches across himself or herself to place the puzzle pieces. Any patterns of oral or written perseveration should also be noted. Of course, the important issue in examining any behavioral pattern or characteristic is determining which behaviors affect the student's interactions with academic requirements and social skills.

Strategies

Strategies are the techniques or rules that a student uses to solve problems and independently complete tasks. It is important to determine what types of strategies a student uses and whether the student can learn or develop new strategies. Sometimes a student may approach tasks very strategically yet elect to use strategies that are ineffective or inappropriate. Students with Asperger Syndrome frequently persist in using unsuccessful strategies simply because they know no replacement strategies for the given situation.

Following written and oral directions is another important strategic thinking component. Many students with Asperger Syndrome find it difficult to organize or prioritize multilevel instructions and require brief, small instructional steps for successful task completion.

It is also important to consider the types of metacognitive strategies that a student applies. Metacognitive strategies include skills such as self-talk, self-monitoring, and self-correction. For example, a young child who is helping her parent make lunch for her family may use a metacognitive strategy. As she makes sandwiches, she may verbally direct herself by saying, "First I spread the peanut butter on the bread, and then I get out the jelly." Children with Asperger Syndrome may never have rehearsed these typical activities (e.g., making a sandwich) and therefore must experience them through direct instructional procedures.

Table 2.4 provides a noninclusive list of sample student learning traits.

Levels of Skill Acquisition

Levels of skill acquisition must be considered when planning the assessment of a student with Asperger Syndrome. Specifically, assessment should occur at the following levels of acquisition: recognition, recall, and application. These levels, which were adapted from instructional levels of presentation (Hudson et al., 1984), are hierarchical, with recognition representing the lowest level of acquisition and application the highest level. If an examiner can determine at which level a student has demonstrated skill mastery, instruction can be appropriately planned.

Table 2.4
Student Learning Traits

I. Learning and Memory

How students approach instruction by focusing their attention and storing information. How complex a pattern can the student perform?

A. Sequential learner

B. Simultaneous learner

C. Stimulus selectivity

D. Attention to detail

E. Memory skills

   1. Short-term

   2. Long-term

   3. Visual

   4. Auditory

   5. Rote

   6. Meaningful

F. Pacing

G. Performance rate

H. Incidental learning

I. Independent work habits

J. Generalization

II. Strategies

Techniques, principles, or rules that allow students to complete tasks independently and solve problems successfully. How are novel tasks approached? How does the student solve problems already known? How does the student organize information?

A. Strategic learner

B. Memory strategies

C. Problem-solving strategies

   1. Academic

   2. Social

D. Metacognitive strategies

   1. Organizational

   2. Self-talk

   3. Self-monitoring

   4. Self-correction

(continues)

Table 2.4
Student Learning Traits *Continued.*

II. **Strategies** *Continued.*

    E. Following oral directions

    F. Following written directions

III. **Behavioral Patterns and Characteristics**

How students apply retrieved information to daily functioning. Which behaviors affect interactions with academic requirements and social skills?

    A. Group interactions

    B. Peer relationships

    C. Adult relationships

    D. Avoidance behaviors

    E. Attention-seeking behaviors

    F. Self-stimulatory behaviors

    G. Response to reinforcement

    H. Response to structure

    I. Response to stressors

    J. Response to success

    K. On-task and off-task behavior

    L. Flexibility or inflexibility

    M. Impulsive behavior

    N. Compulsive behavior

    O. Echolalia

    P. Perseveration (oral, motor, or written)

    Q. Dominance

    R. Perseverance

    S. Distractibility

    T. Eye contact

    U. Excessive movement

    V. Sense of humor

    W. Self-concept

To assess the recognition level, an examiner might ask a student with Asperger Syndrome to select a stimulus item from similar distractors. At this level of skill acquisition, the student is not expected to generate the correct response without cues but rather only to discriminate an item from similar stimuli through a written or oral response. Assessment activities at the recognition level include multiple-choice or matching items. These activities allow students to respond through pointing, underlining, circling, or matching appropriate items. Students who successfully perform recognition-level tasks typically demonstrate readiness to generate original thought relative to that task.

Assessment at the recall level involves asking students to retrieve information or perform tasks without stimulus clues. At this level, students generate thoughts, ideas, or concepts, responding orally or in writing to assessment items. Activities that assess skill acquisition at the recall level include fill-in-the-blank, flash card, or short-answer items. The student who successfully completes a task at the recall level is prepared to apply rote information in a more meaningful manner.

The application level of skill acquisition represents the meaningful use of a skill in a simulated or contrived setting. Assessment tasks are structured so that students can demonstrate proficiency in the classroom or other setting. The importance of application-level assessment was seen in the movie *Rain Man* (Guber, Peters, & Levinson, 1988). In this movie Raymond Babbitt, a man with autism played by Dustin Hoffman, demonstrated a unique ability with numbers. He could perform recall-level tasks in mathematics, specifically, adding, subtracting, multiplying, and dividing large numbers without the aid of a calculator or response cues. However, when asked to apply numerical skills to a real-life setting (i.e., use numbers to indicate an understanding of money), his lack of application skills was evident. Assessment tasks at the application level include word problems, theme writing, and comprehending and following written directions.

Levels of Instructional Representation

Many of the current practices in cognitive development and education are based on the developmental theories of Jean Piaget (1959). From Piaget's description of the type of knowledge displayed by children at various stages of development from birth to adulthood, Bruner (1966) specified three levels of representation through which a child must progress to become an independent learner. The first stage is the concrete, or enactive, during which the student is actively and physically involved in a learning task. Many children learn best by "doing," whether learning to ride a bicycle or learning the concept of place value in math. In either case, the student interacts with a physical object—the bicycle or place-value manipulatives (e.g., blocks)— to gain a concrete understanding of the process. At this level, the student develops a schema, or pattern, that becomes the basis for future knowledge.

The second, or iconic, stage involves the use of graphics or images to prompt the student to retrieve the prior knowledge needed to complete a task or solve a problem. A common iconic instructional presentation is the use of pictures or diagrams in math. Most students who used blocks to grasp the concept of place value should be able to respond to items illustrated with drawings of blocks. Bruner (1966) described this stage as governed by principles of perceptual organization.

Symbolic, the final stage, involves representation in language or words. Students at this level of representation have developed a schema based on past experiences with a task and are able to respond appropriately to symbols (e.g., words) on a page without further prompts or clues. For instance, a student given a math problem involving regrouping for addition or subtraction will recall his prior experience with place value and apply that knowledge to computing the answer.

Normal development proceeds sequentially through the three stages; however, students with Asperger Syndrome may have gaps in their knowledge, resulting in splinter skills. For example, they may have developed the ability to work with abstract symbols without understanding the underlying concepts or being able to work with concrete manipulatives.

When assessing students with Asperger Syndrome for purposes of instructional planning, examiners should determine whether students are able to demonstrate comprehension on all three levels: concrete, iconic, and symbolic. Examiners must assess students' understanding of underlying concepts, as well as their ability to respond to written problems at an abstract level. Students who have a great deal of rote knowledge or who have developed a successful strategy for test taking may do relatively well on written tests but be deficient in concrete, conceptual understanding needed to build a solid academic knowledge base. Accordingly, teachers and diagnosticians should schedule at least some assessment at the concrete and iconic levels, areas typically not examined beyond the primary grades.

Diagnostic Teaching

As with student learning traits, the focus of diagnostic teaching is listening to the student, understanding what he or she feels, and interpreting the subsequent interactions within the learning environment. Thus, diagnostic teaching is a systematic, clinical process in which the student is presented with a task or series of tasks that are new. The student is asked to solve a problem or complete an activity while the examiner notes observations and maintains anecdotal records. These notes should describe how the student approaches the task, deals with task frustration, and modifies and self-corrects errors, as well as what problem-solving skills the student uses while completing the task. As the diagnostic teaching session progresses, the examiner may offer clues or suggestions and even teach small components needed to complete the task.

Another application of diagnostic teaching involves presenting similar tasks to the student using a variety of presentation or response modes. For example, six spelling words, all unfamiliar to the student and similar in structure and difficulty, are presented for practice using three different modalities. The student practices two words verbally by spelling each word aloud and then using the word in a sentence. The student practices another two words in a written format by writing each word 10 times. The student practices the final two words kinesthetically, or tactilely, by drawing the letters in a box of damp sand. Each practice session lasts approximately 3 minutes. At the conclusion of the practice sessions, the student is tested, for the same type of response required in his or her classroom. The results are then compared to see if different practice modes facilitated the student's memorization of the spelling words. Common presentation and response modes used in this type of diagnostic teaching include visual, auditory, tactile or kinesthetic, and combinations of two or more of these modalities.

Diagnostic teaching sessions are usually brief, lasting 15 minutes or less. Throughout the session, the examiner observes the student's response patterns and notes areas of strength. The practitioner works with the student's strengths, addresses deficit skill areas, introduces compensatory mechanisms, and rearranges home and school environments to meet the student's specific learning needs.

Portfolio Analysis

Portfolio assessment is increasingly seen as an alternative to formal and informal assessment (Duffy, Jones, & Thomas, 1999; Schutt & McCabe, 1994). This type of assessment places students in the role of evaluators. Specifically, the students participate with their teachers in evaluating their skills and selecting assignments or projects that reflect their current skill level (Hendrick-Keefe, 1995). Using portfolio assessment promotes accountability in both the teacher and student. This person-centered assessment is strength driven, concentrating on academic gains rather then deficits (Carlson, Hagiwara, & Quinn, 1998; Swicegood, 1994). In addition, students who prepare portfolios gain management skills and acquire ownership in their portfolios by determining, with the instructor, what will be included.

The following items should be included in a portfolio: (a) a table of contents or sections detailing what is included in the portfolio, (b) an explanation of the included materials and why they were selected, (c) behavior and adaptive functioning data, (d) strategic learning and self-regulation data, and (e) academic or daily living skills data. Work samples included in the portfolio should be selected from a variety of classes (Hendrick-Keefe, 1995; Swicegood, 1994).

Although little research has been conducted on using portfolio assessment with students with Asperger Syndrome, the combination of quantitative and qualitative data it yields may assist in providing a more comprehensive picture of a student's functional abilities. In addition, portfolios may initiate positive instructor–student–family interactions, while providing students with valuable decision-making opportunities (Carlson et al., 1998; Duffy et al., 1999; Hendrick-Keefe, 1995; Swicegood, 1994).

Ecobehavioral Assessment

Ecobehavioral assessment provides information on a student's behavior through manipulation of the environment and other ecological factors (Carlson et al., 1998; Gable, Hendrickson, & Sealander, 1997; Kamps, Leonard, Dugan, Boland, & Greenwood, 1991). Its intent is "to capture not only the instructional context(s) in which the problems [behaviors] occur, but also the exact nature of student academic performance and classroom deportment" (Gable et al., 1997, p. 25). Thus, ecobehavioral assessment examines both the behavior and the ecological factors that support it. The educator who uses this method observes several lessons to identify types of instruction that occur when a behavior problem is present, the student's performance on academic tasks, and the classroom structure. The teacher can document the co-occurrence of student behavior, academic demands, and classroom structure. Gable and colleagues suggest looking at the following ecological variables or task requirements: (a) paper and pencil, (b) lecture, (c) teacher–pupil discussion, (d) manipulatives, (e) instructional games, (f) workbooks or worksheets, (g) basals or other reading materials, (h) student-to-student discussion, (i) media or technology, and (j) transition. Ecological assessment requires a great deal of examiner time but can yield useful information about instructional practices and setting demands that can significantly affect a student's success (Conroy & Fox, 1994).

Translating Assessment Results into Meaningful Procedures

After conducting observations, scoring protocols, and analyzing test results, the examiner must synthesize the data to clarify the student's performance status. Synthesis is the interpretation and integration of findings or information. A synthesis of assessment results describes the meaning of test results or observations and provides insight into how this information can affect instructional strategies. According to Carlson et al. (1998), "The synthesis process may well be the most important aspect of any assessment battery. It is customary for a synthesis to be presented as a written report, along with other information such as anecdotal observations, test scores, and recommendations" (p. 44).

Three basic types of statements should be included in the assessment report: information, inferences, and judgments (Moran, 1995). Information is specific and verifiable. An information statement includes only facts about what occurred during testing and observation. Information should be stated as quantifiable outcomes or in concrete terms such as "hit," "kick," and "bite" rather than, say, "aggressive behavior." An example of an information statement is "Andy hit the examiner's right hand three times while attempting the puzzle activity."

Inference statements are less specific than information statements and may include interpretive comments that go beyond the observable facts. Therefore, inferences are more subjective than information and cannot be directly verified. The majority of the synthesis in an assessment report consists of inference statements. For example, if David did not complete five out of six items on a particular subtest, the examiner could infer that David did not possess the necessary skills to perform at that skill level.

Judgment statements are usually contained in the final section of the assessment report. They are both general and subjective. Thus, judgment statements can be recommendations or diagnoses that combine inferences and information. For example, a judgment statement might be "Diane should receive reading instruction in a one-on-one setting specially designed for students with Asperger Syndrome."

Strengths and concerns should be clearly delineated in an assessment report. It is recommended that a two-column format be used for the list of strengths and concerns. In one column, the specific strength or concern is listed; in the other column, evidence is provided (Carlson et al., 1998). For example, when the examiner writes "answers inferential questions at the first-grade level" in the concern column, he or she provides direct evidence for the concern, such as "answered incorrectly three inferential questions in two first-grade texts that were silently read by the student," in the other column.

Acknowledging student strengths is also important in developing an educational plan. Detailing the student's strengths is especially helpful in developing an educational plan that fosters the student's knowledge and skills. For example, if a student can use various computer programs, the examiner can make a recommendation such as "Provide Johnny opportunities to use various computer programs and gradually shift him to helping others use the computer."

The examiner compiles the aforementioned information in an assessment report, including protocols, copies of relevant articles, or other materials that would be helpful to those implementing the recommendations made by the examiner. In addition, the examiner plans the agenda for a meeting of those concerned and schedules the meeting (Carlson et al., 1998).

At the meeting, the examiner should create a positive, interactive atmosphere. According to Moran (1995), all parties at the meeting should (a) have a mutual respect for each participant's competency, (b) realize that each person has a unique but equally valuable skill to offer, (c) regard all participants as equals, and (d) remain flexible about recommendations. Participants may have difficulty understanding specific terminology related to the assessment process and the different disciplines represented at the meeting. The examiner can avoid misinterpretations by clarifying terminology and avoiding professional jargon. It is important that all participants feel comfortable and welcome to make suggestions and discuss personal perspectives.

The assessment interpretation can be a valuable tool for creating individualized interventions. For parents it may serve an additional function to decrease anxiety about their child's exceptionality. For the individual with Asperger Syndrome, this meeting may increase self-awareness of strengths and challenges. This meeting also provides professionals and parents involved in the student's educational plan an opportunity to share different perspectives and creates an atmosphere of a team working toward a similar goal—to help the individual with Asperger Syndrome meet his potential (Carlson et al., 1998).

When assessment allows for a thorough investigation of a student's strengths and concerns, it becomes a useful tool for developing educational intervention strategies. For students with Asperger Syndrome, assessment provides a direct link for establishing quality service, because many of these students do not function well in the classroom without individualized curricula. Students with Asperger Syndrome demonstrate a wide range of discrepancies in skills and capabilities. Many have limited generalization abilities and unique information-processing functions. Teachers and other professionals are required to provide educational services that are precisely matched with the individual's needs. Therefore, integration of educational intervention and thorough, ongoing assessment enables individualized educational services for students with Asperger Syndrome (Carlson et al., 1998).

It is not a simple task to establish a routine of assessment-based intervention in daily school life. Assessment-based intervention begins with an examination of the student's specific strengths and concerns as revealed by the evaluation. The professional draws on the strengths to establish short- and long-range objectives to address deficits. The professional uses feedback on preferred teaching styles and response modes to select and develop curriculum and instructional procedures. The process concludes where it began—with a continual reexamination of the individual's skills and abilities and modifications to the intervention procedures. Thus, the cycle of testing, teaching, and modifying continues throughout the student's educational life.

Concluding Thoughts

Many different types of assessment procedures are available for students with Asperger Syndrome. Professionals must select a battery of measures most appropriate for each individual student. Norm-referenced tests and developmental assessments are suitable for initial diagnosis, periodic comprehensive overview, and summative evaluation. Informal assessment techniques can be chosen for daily or ongoing formative evaluation of student skills. Finally, ecobehavioral measures allow for physical and interactive modifications to the learning environment. Together, these tools can yield a comprehensive picture of a student's abilities and needs, allowing practitioners and families to work collaboratively to create the optimal learning environment for the student with Asperger Syndrome.

Teaching Academic Content to Students with Asperger Syndrome

3

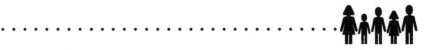

S chool is a complex environment that requires students to use cognitive, social, behavioral, and motor skills to prosper and grow. Students with Asperger Syndrome have many strengths, particularly in the cognitive domain, that can contribute to school success; however, when cognitive demands are paired with other environmental demands (e.g., social demands, organizational skills), these students' achievement may not parallel their potential. Students with Asperger Syndrome also have very specific talents; they tend to excel when they are given concrete, visual stimuli but experience problems when abstractions are used. The social nature of the school environment also requires consideration. Students with Asperger Syndrome often want to interact with others but often do not understand the rules of social relationships. Thus, the environment makes a variety of structural, academic, and social demands, many of which are not well defined. Students with Asperger Syndrome have difficulty coping with each of these demands individually; when they are combined, school can become a confusing, frustrating, and sometimes frightening place.

Characteristics That Affect Academic Performance

Students with Asperger Syndrome are typically of average or above-average intelligence. In fact, IQs of persons with Asperger Syndrome have been documented in the gifted range (Barnhill,

Hagiwara, Myles, & Simpson, 2000). Because of their IQ level, students with Asperger Syndrome are often expected to perform at the same level as their peers. Although some students can meet this expectation, many cannot. It is often difficult for teachers to detect that students may not be completing their work in a meaningful way. As mentioned in Chapter 2, these students are able to mask their inability to understand and perform certain tasks. Because their disabilities are usually confounded by their abilities, students with Asperger Syndrome give the impression that they are competent in many skill areas in which they actually have deficits.

It is difficult to identify the specific areas of ability and disability of persons with Asperger Syndrome because of their heterogeneity, or the diversity of their abilities and disabilities. A person with Asperger Syndrome may exhibit problems in two, three, four, or even more areas of functioning. Furthermore, these deficits may be moderate to severe.

The goal of this chapter is to give an overview of some areas of academic functioning that may be impaired in persons with Asperger Syndrome. Instructional strategies that can enhance academic success are also discussed.

Distraction and Inattention

Persons with Asperger Syndrome often receive a diagnosis of attention-deficit/hyperactivity disorder (ADHD) at some point in their lives. The conditions have many commonalities, particularly related to distractibility and inattentiveness. Attention often seems fleeting. One moment, the student with Asperger Syndrome may appear to be paying attention, then suddenly seems to withdraw into an inner world and be totally unaware of the environment. Teacher directions are not processed; student conversations are not heard. This daydreaming may occur over extended periods, with no predictability. The daydreaming is often so intense that a physical prompt from the teacher is needed to call the student back to task. Often the antecedent is unknown.

Even while paying attention, the student may not react to teacher instructions. For example, the student may start to follow a three-step direction but appear to lose focus as he completes the first phase. Rather than looking for a model or asking for help, the student looks for a way out. The student may remain frozen in that place, wander aimlessly about, shuffle through the desk, stare into space, or begin to daydream. On occasion, the student may cause a distraction or act out. Often these same behaviors are seen when the student is required to engage in nonpreferred work tasks for extended periods.

Social interactions are often distracting for students with Asperger Syndrome. Because these students want to interact with others in general, they often focus all of their attention on others in the classroom instead of on the tasks at hand. If the student with Asperger Syndrome has a particularly strong need to interact with a specific classmate, she may attend to that person exclusively, staring nonstop at the person or listening to that person's conversations. If the student with Asperger Syndrome and the classmate have developed a reciprocal relationship, the student with Asperger Syndrome might unilaterally seek the classmate's approval before beginning a task or addressing the teacher or another student. This gives the peer an enormous amount of power over the person with Asperger Syndrome, which can be used in a negative way. For example, the peer may prompt the student with Asperger Syndrome to complete assignments for him, ask the student to break classroom rules, or prompt the student to engage in activities that will place her in harm's way.

Students with Asperger Syndrome are often distracted because they do not know how to discern relevant from irrelevant stimuli. A student with Asperger Syndrome might focus on a particular picture or map in a textbook while other students in the class have moved on to the next chapter. This student might focus on the way a speaker's earring dangles when she moves her head instead of listening to the content of her lecture. The student with Asperger Syndrome may become highly frustrated when she attempts to memorize every fact associated with Columbus's discovering America as mentioned in the textbook, including an extensive list of food and supplies carried on each ship. The student does not innately know that memorizing such information is not necessary.

Tunnel Vision

School requires that students attend to certain stimuli while screening out irrelevant yet competing distractions. That is, at any given time a student might be expected to attend to a textbook and ignore (a) students talking around her, (b) a teacher offering another student help, or (c) a bulletin board about a favored topic. This is often difficult for the student with Asperger Syndrome for several reasons.

On one level, the student with Asperger Syndrome often cannot discern what others deem relevant. If the bulletin board contains information on a topic of high interest, the student may consider it more important than a text. If a student with Asperger Syndrome has a strong social attachment to someone across the room, interacting with that person might take precedence over any task the teacher assigns. Rational explanations that talking across the room is inappropriate may not affect the student with Asperger Syndrome. This student might seem "driven" to interact with his friend.

Tunnel vision also operates in a second way. Students with Asperger Syndrome logically group items or characteristics so that they make sense to them. That is, they form a schema that is exact and often inflexible. For example, a student who learns the spelling rule "*i* before *e* except after *c*" might apply the rule rigidly. The student would be convinced that words like *neighbor* and *weigh* should be spelled *nieghbor* and *wiegh*.

Problems can present themselves when the student is reading for information. Generally, reading for information is a difficult task. Students with Asperger Syndrome are most likely to read for specific information presented in a text study guide while ignoring and simply not processing in a meaningful way information that they were not responsible for. When the student is later tested on the text and given questions that were not in the study guide, he will most likely not answer those questions or answer them incorrectly, even if the information seems obvious to others.

Student obsessions are another hallmark of tunnel vision. Two types of obsessions are typically exhibited by students with Asperger Syndrome. The first type of obsession (primary) is one where the student has an all-encompassing level of interest in a particular topic. As a result, a discussion of this topic can escalate to uncontrollable, almost tantrumlike behavior. Rapid speech, increased volume, a high-pitched voice, pacing, and hand-wringing often occur with primary obsessions. Primary obsessions typically do not lend themselves to rational discussions and explorations. Indeed, students who have this type of obsession seem to discuss the topic in an almost circular fashion.

Secondary obsessions, on the other hand, are marked interests about which the student remains lucid, focused, and ready to learn about the particular topic. Students actively seek new information about the topic but can be somewhat easily redirected. Secondary interests are often used by teachers to motivate students to complete academic tasks. In some cases, secondary obsessions develop into career interests.

Some professionals who work with students with Asperger Syndrome speculate that distraction, inattention, and tunnel vision are prominent features of this disability—that these factors are the overriding characteristics that affect and influence the other deficit areas. Although these professionals acknowledge that rote memory may be a problem, they maintain that it is in large part due to the distraction, inattention, and tunnel vision that occur when students attempt to use their rote memory skills.

Rote Memory

Rote memory skills are generally well developed in persons with Asperger Syndrome. Case studies document that some children have learned to recite words they see written by age 3. Others have reported that young children with Asperger Syndrome have been able to repeat paragraphs of information after seeing them only once. However, the comprehension level of many of these persons does not appear to match their rote skills. Comprehension is often at the factual level. That is, persons with Asperger Syndrome can understand basic facts in written material and either repeat them verbatim or paraphrase them. Many, however, experience difficulty understanding vocabulary in context and reading for information. Thus, persons with Asperger Syndrome may give the false impression that they understand concepts because they are able to parrot responses. As a result, it is easy for a teacher to mistake rote responses for content mastery and urge the student to master more difficult material. Students may be able to repeat algebra equations but be unable to perform them. Similarly, they may be able to answer multiple-choice questions about a novel they have read but be unable to analyze character intent in a cooperative group setting.

Rote memory may be nonproductive for students with Asperger Syndrome in another way. Educators assume that a good rote memory means that students can remember, at any time, pieces of information or events. This is not true for many persons with Asperger Syndrome, however. Although they can store chunks of information in memory, they often have difficulty determining how to retrieve the information. Open-ended questions such as "Tell me what the main character in the story did after his horse disappeared" may not trigger a response, because the student has stored the information under the main character's name and is unable to make the transition from the term *main character* to the character's name. In most students with Asperger Syndrome, therefore, an exceptional memory is not related to the ability to recall information.

A third way in which rote memory may be nonproductive in persons with Asperger Syndrome is related to integration of learned material and experience. These students may memorize entire inventories of facts or directions, but these lists often remain unconnected bits of information. For example, a student with Asperger Syndrome might memorize the list of supplies to bring to each of his six middle-school classes and recite them when supplied with the appropriate trigger or key word. This same student might forget, however, to bring a pencil to class. Another student might remember to bring a pencil to class but arrive with it unsharpened. She knows from past experience that the pencil must have a point to be a useful tool but somehow does not connect this bit of information to her present need. Although by adolescence these students have memorized innumerable bits of academic information, their knowledge tends to be fragmented and of limited utility.

Visual Versus Auditory Processing

Many students with Asperger Syndrome learn and process information in a manner that is generally incompatible with the way academic information is presented. Most academic information is presented orally, but students with Asperger Syndrome often have difficulty with auditory input (Dunn, Myles, & Orr, 2002; Rinner, 2000). Processing difficulties may occur for one of three reasons.

First, the student can understand and follow directions in sentences and, indeed, understands sentences if additional processing time is given. However, because the words are presented orally, the student has no time in which to reflect.

Second, the student may understand individual words used by a teacher or student but not understand what the words mean when they are used in the context of sentences and paragraphs. The student requires additional processing time to understand the meaning of the words as they are used in sentences. If the student attempts to memorize the words using rote memory skills, it is almost as if there is little cognitive energy left with which to process meaning.

Third, it is speculated that, when asked to process visual and auditory information concurrently, students with Asperger Syndrome are often unable to do so. Information must be presented in one modality or the other to facilitate processing; otherwise, overload occurs.

Structure

Students with Asperger Syndrome typically fall at the ends of the structure continuum: They either have an inherent ability to provide structure or rely totally on others to help them organize themselves. It is often said that students with Asperger Syndrome have either the neatest or messiest desks in class.

Generally, it is easier for persons with Asperger Syndrome to function in an organized environment. Predictable schedules, uniform assignment formats, and consistent teacher affect help these students devote their time and energy to academic tasks. Those who have internal structure often have rigid expectations that schedules be followed and commitments be honored; unscheduled events cause these students great discomfort that can be manifested as disorientation, refusal to engage in the new activity, extended discourse about the canceled or postponed event, or behavioral problems. In other words, the student communicates through language and behavior that change is difficult.

Educators comment that they have seen students with Asperger Syndrome tolerate change in some instances but lose control when the environment was altered. Sometimes students with Asperger Syndrome can tolerate change if that change occurs in only one dimension. For example, if library time is changed, the student may adjust to the new schedule. However, if library time and the librarian are changed simultaneously, the same student may have difficulty maintaining any type of self-control.

Most students with Asperger Syndrome have limited ability to structure their own environment. A messy person with Asperger Syndrome probably has not made a conscious choice to be that way; rather, he or she lacks good organizational skills. A student with this disability can literally lose a paper received only a minute earlier. He never has a pencil in class. The note that the teacher placed in the student's backpack never makes it home. Written work is not placed uniformly on a page. A middle-school student's locker is a mess; she often cannot locate her locker combination, and when she does, she cannot find what she needs inside. She cannot organize her day by bringing her science and math books to science class, even though math class follows immediately in the room next door. Almost every facet of the student's life is in disarray. Teachers and parents often wonder how the student gets from one place to another. It is a challenge to organize this type of student. Merely providing a schedule or list of supplies is not enough, because these aids are most often lost.

Problem Solving

Although students with Asperger Syndrome are often able to engage in high-level thinking and problem solving when their area of interest is involved, these skills are often not generalized throughout the school day. Many students select one problem-solving strategy and use it consistently regardless of the situation. Persistence is common in persons with Asperger Syndrome. For example, if the school locker does not open, the student may keep trying the combination. Although this strategy can be effective, there needs to be a self-monitoring component. If the student has tried the combination five times unsuccessfully, chances are that there is another problem with the locker. Persistence, if unsuccessful, may result in a behavioral outburst if the student does not know the problem-solving strategy of asking an adult or peer for help when difficulty arises.

Other students with Asperger Syndrome may have learned several problem-solving strategies but not have generalized their use. For example, the student with Asperger Syndrome may know to use a dictionary to find a word meaning in English class but not realize that the same technique may also be effective in understanding a term in science.

There is also the problem of recall related to problem solving. Although a student may know a host of problem-solving strategies and realize that they can be generalized, he may not be able to recall any strategies when they are needed. Because the student with Asperger Syndrome often has difficulty searching his or her memory for particular facts, the student may not be able to access a strategy. Even if the student has an effective system for retrieving problem-solving strategies, it is still likely that he cannot consistently use this system. By the time the student cognitively realizes that a problem exists, he is typically so confused, angry, or disoriented that his reaction is behavioral—a tantrum or withdrawal.

Problem solving becomes even more difficult in academics if abstract concepts are involved. Students with Asperger Syndrome frequently have difficulty with word problems, estimation, algebra, and geometry—all of which require problem-solving skills and often contain a high level of abstraction.

Problem-solving difficulties are also apparent outside the field of mathematics. Teachers often give assignments that require students to take the role of a historical character. Students often write papers or plays or make speeches as a historical figure. Tasks of this nature are difficult for those who do not understand the human experience from different perspectives. Persons with Asperger Syndrome have difficulty understanding their own state of mind; therefore, they cannot be expected to imagine the state of mind of others.

Motor Skills

Motor problems that are often seen in persons with Asperger Syndrome affect academic performance. Specifically, students with Asperger Syndrome are often clumsy, have an unusual gait, have difficulty with pencil grasp, and write illegibly. Gross motor problems may lead to fear of heights and inability to jump over obstacles, skip, or catch or throw a ball. Fine motor difficulties mean that students may not be motivated to complete work because of the enormous amount of energy required to write. Students who consent to write often turn in assignments that are unreadable. As a result, they are often told to rewrite the page and try to be neater. Requests like this result in negative reactions. Depending on the student's behavioral repertoire, reactions may include refusal to do the task, withdrawal, ignoring the teacher, daydreaming, or an overt display directed toward self, peers, or the teacher.

Motivation

Students with Asperger Syndrome are often not motivated to complete a task just because it was assigned by the teacher. If the task does not make sense in the scheme of the student's life, chances are he or she will see no reason to invest time and energy. "When will I use algebra, anyway?" is a frequent question. Teacher statements such as "You need to do it because I said so" often do not have the desired impact on the student with Asperger Syndrome. Even if the task has relevance to everyday life, the student may not make that connection.

Engaging a student in extensive rhetoric to convince him of the importance of the assignment may not be effective for several reasons. Even if the student is apt to listen to the teacher's explanation, he may not understand the abstract concepts used by the teacher to link the assignment with "real life" needs. Another student with Asperger Syndrome may like the teacher rhetoric because the focus is removed from the task at hand and the student does not have to complete the assignment, at least in the short run.

Obsessions, particularly secondary obsessions, often serve as effective motivators for students with Asperger Syndrome. Once a topic of interest is identified, the student appears to spend the majority of time reflecting and acting on it in a somewhat rational and lucid manner. As a result, the student is typically highly motivated to learn more about the area of obsession and is anxious to share knowledge with others. That this information sharing occurs regardless of the interest level of the listeners, however, can sometimes be a problem.

Individuals with Asperger Syndrome are often motivated by people they like; conversely, they may refuse to engage in activities or complete tasks if they involve people with whom they would rather not interact. Thus, it is important that students with Asperger Syndrome be assigned to teachers who have the potential to develop positive, reciprocal relationships with them.

Motivation is also linked to the student's mistaken impression that he or she has control over a variety of situations. When the teacher announces that everyone did poorly on the spelling test, it is not uncommon for a student with Asperger Syndrome to think that she is to blame. Egocentricity dictates that the person with Asperger Syndrome be at the center of most events and directly affect the performance of others. There may be a profound sense of burden because the student feels at fault.

Effective Instructional Strategies

Students with Asperger Syndrome have endless potential when teachers recognize their individual needs and characteristics and structure the environment for success. Use of priming, assignment modifications, and enrichment activities can enhance the performance of individuals with Asperger Syndrome.

Priming

Priming refers to the introduction of information, assignments, or activities prior to their use (Wilde, Koegel, & Koegel, 1992). The purposes of priming are consistent with the needs of students with Asperger Syndrome. For these students, who react to surprises or unexpected activities with stress and anxiety and thrive on predictability, priming (a) familiarizes the individual with the material before its use; (b) introduces predictability into the information or activity, thereby reducing stress and anxiety; and (c) increases the likelihood of success (Myles & Adreon, 2001).

According to Wilde and colleagues (1992), the actual materials that will be used in a lesson should be shown to the student the day, the evening, or even the morning before the activity is to take place. The student is reinforced for attending to the material. In some cases, priming occurs right before the activity, such as when a paraprofessional overviews what will take place during a cooperative group activity immediately prior to the beginning of class. Priming can be done by a parent at home or by a paraprofessional, a resource teacher, or a trusted peer (Myles & Adreon, 2001).

Wilde et al. (1992) also recommended that the actual materials, such as a worksheet or textbook, be used in priming. However, in some cases, a list or a description of the activities to take place may suffice. For students, priming may consist of reviewing an index card that has a reading assignment, identifying the number and type of questions to answer, determining how instruction will occur (in a small group of peers or individually), and defining responsibilities for each class (Myles & Adreon, 2001).

Assignment Modifications

There are several considerations when giving assignments to children and youth with Asperger Syndrome. Specifically, attention to length of the assignment is often warranted. Even though they have average or above average intelligence, many students with Asperger Syndrome require additional processing time to complete assignments or write slowly because of fine motor problems. In addition, these students can show competence of concepts after completing a few items. It is often in the best interest of the student and teacher to match the number of items that should be completed to the time available and the student's rate. Assignments that are modified in length are successful for many individuals with Asperger Syndrome.

As previously stated, assignments that require lengthy written documentation can be problematic for children and youth with Asperger Syndrome. Offering alternatives to paper-and-pencil tasks allows students to demonstrate their knowledge and often serves as a motivator. Winebrenner (2001) listed several alternatives to traditional assignments, including (a) creating a radio or televised newscast, (b) creating a script or mock trial, (c) surveying others and making a graph of the outcomes, (d) creating a diary or journal surrounding an important event, and (e) developing a timeline. Other modifications, centered around changing the format of assignments, include verbal responses instead of written essays and multiple-choice rather than short-answer tests (Myles & Adreon, 2001).

Attention must also be paid to the amount of reading required of students with Asperger Syndrome, particularly at the middle and high school levels. Although some individuals with

Asperger Syndrome are voracious readers when motivated, they may take significantly longer than peers to complete reading assignments. Providing texts that are highlighted and study guides can help students maximize their reading time. Teachers should also identify for students the specific content that they are responsible for learning (Myles & Adreon, 2001). In bringing attention to relevant material, teachers should also provide a model of assignments so that students have a visual reminder of how their tasks should look.

Enrichment

Too little attention has been paid to providing enrichment to individuals with Asperger Syndrome (Myles & Adreon, 2001). Research has shown that more individuals with Asperger Syndrome have superior to very superior intelligence than do individuals in the neurotypical population (Barnhill, Hagiwara, Myles, & Simpson, 2000). Assessment of district or school competencies can be helpful in identifying the content that students with Asperger Syndrome already know. If students already know the content to be presented, that time could be devoted to enrichment activities, including a focus on special interest areas (Myles & Adreon, 2001).

Structural Strategies

Structural strategies as well as an appropriate instructional sequence can help students with Asperger Syndrome attend to and profit from instruction. Appropriate environmental strategies include (a) visual supports, (b) preparation for changes in routine, (c) a buddy program, (d) early or late release, (e) assignment notebooks, (f) timelines, (g) the Travel Card, and (h) home base.

Visual Supports

As previously mentioned, students with Asperger Syndrome benefit when information is presented visually rather than orally. Visual information is more concrete than auditory information and allows for greater processing time. Visual schedules, graphic organizers, outlines, and task cards can help individuals with Asperger Syndrome understand content and carry out assignments.

Visual Schedules. Visual schedules take an abstract concept such as time and present it in a more concrete and manageable form. They can yield multiple benefits for children and youth with Asperger Syndrome, who often exhibit visual strengths. For example, visual schedules allow students to anticipate upcoming events and activities, develop an understanding of time, and predict change. Furthermore, they can be used to stimulate communication through discussion of past, present, and future events; increase on-task behavior; facilitate transition between activities; and teach new skills.

Visual schedules are based on the strengths and needs of the student. Depending on the student's characteristics, a visual schedule may be based on levels of visual representation. As would be expected, the more abstract the visual schedule, the higher the level of representation. Table 3.1 represents the hierarchy of visual representation from the highest to the lowest level of abstraction.

For young students who require concrete visual cues to understand upcoming events, the teacher can design an object schedule that uses the actual materials from each of the scheduled activities. For example, if a math lesson requires the use of colored blocks as manipulatives, then the colored blocks may be used to represent math.

Older, more advanced students may benefit from schedules that use colored drawings of the student completing the activity, black-and-white line drawings, written words, or sentences. It is important to determine which level of visual representation is

TABLE 3.1
Level of Abstraction for Visual Schedules

Level of Abstraction	Visual Representation
highest	written phrase or sentence
↑	written word
	black-and-white line drawing
	colored drawing
	photograph
↓	miniature object
lowest	full-sized object

appropriate for each student and then pair it with the next highest level. For example, if a student is functioning at the photograph level, a colored drawing can be paired with the photograph to introduce the higher level concept. Similarly, if a student is functioning at the black-and-white drawing level, written words can be paired with the drawing.

Schedule arrangement and placement options vary by student need and level of functioning. Schedules can be arranged left to right or top to bottom. Although either arrangement is acceptable, the left-to-right arrangement facilitates behavior required for reading. Schedules can take a variety of forms, including the following:

- placing the schedule in a photo album or three-ring binder

- hanging the schedule on the classroom wall with Velcro or masking tape

- placing the schedule in a pocket chart

- writing the schedule on a wipe-off board

- writing the schedule on a chalkboard

- typing the schedule on a piece of paper and placing it on the student's desk

- typing the schedule on an index card that will fit in the student's pocket or wallet

- writing the schedule on hole-punched cards that can hang on the student's belt loop with an O-ring

Students may enjoy and sometimes feel more comfortable when participating in the preparation of their schedule. This participation should occur first thing in the morning. Students can assist in assembling their schedule, copying it, or adding their own personal touch. This interactive time can also be used to review the daily routine, discuss changes, and reinforce rules.

Figures 3.1a, 3.1b, and 3.2 provide samples of visual schedules. The first schedule was designed for a younger student with Asperger Syndrome who requires a moderate level of abstraction to understand the day's events. The second schedule is appropriate for students who have a high level of abstraction but require time and activity cues.

Daily Schedule: Wednesday

Morning	Afternoon
1 Opening	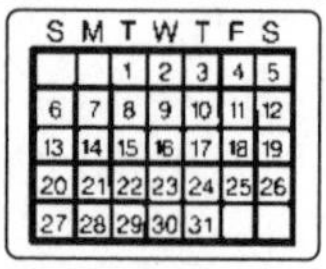 6 Lunch 
2 Reading	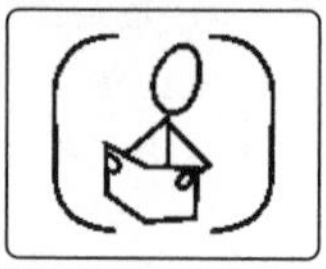 7 P.E. 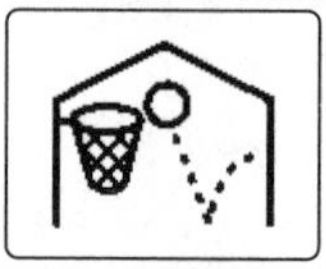
3 Math	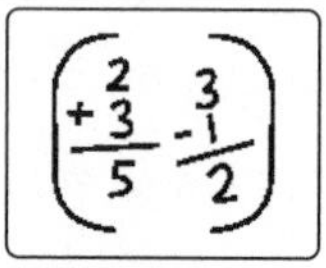 8 Science 
4 Journal	 9 Recess 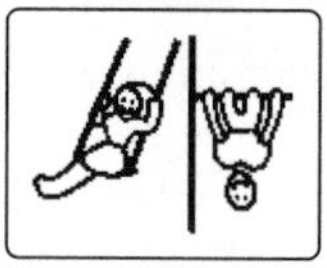
5 Recess	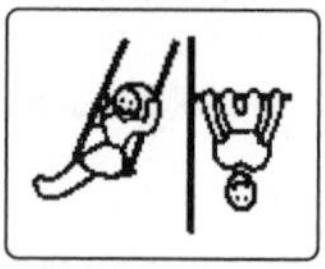 10 Bus 

Figure 3.1a. Sample visual schedules for a student who functions at a moderate level of abstraction. *Note.* Schedules made with the Boardmaker and Picture Communication Symbols. © 1987–2001 by Mayer-Johnson, P.O. Box 1579, Solana Beach, CA 92075, 858/550-0084, fax 858/550-0449, e-mail: mayerj@mayer-johnson.com. Reprinted with permission.

Graphic Organizers. Graphic organizers provide a visual, holistic representation of facts and concepts within an organized framework. Graphic organizers arrange key terms to show their relationship to one another, providing abstract or implicit information in a concrete manner. They are particularly useful with content area material. Graphic organizers can be used before, during, or after students read a selection, either as an advance organizer or as a measure of concept attainment. Graphic

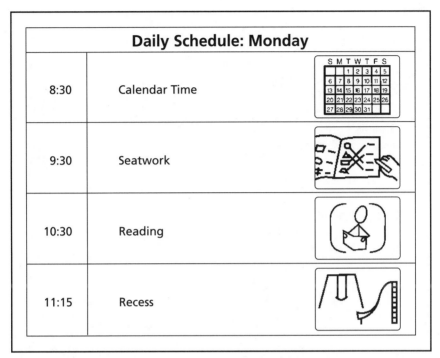

Figure 3.1b. *Continued.*

organizers often enhance the learning of students with Asperger Syndrome because

- the visual modality is often a strength for these students;

- they remain consistent and constant, so when the student "tunes in," they are available for viewing;

- they allow for processing time so the student can reflect on the written material at his or her own pace; and

- they present abstract information in a concrete manner that is often more easily understood than a verbal presentation alone.

One type of graphic organizer is the semantic map. The focal point of the semantic map is the key word or concept enclosed in a geometric figure (e.g., circle or square) or in a pictorial representation of the word or concept. Lines or arrows connect this central

8:00 A.M.	bus routine (put up coat and backpack, use bathroom review schedule with teacher or paraeducator)	
8:15 A.M.	breakfast	
8:30 A.M.	morning group	
9:00 A.M.	math activities	
10:00 A.M.	reading activities	
11:00 A.M.	adaptive physical education	
11:30 A.M.	lunch time	
12:00 P.M.	recess	
12:30 P.M.	work time (prevocational activity)	
1:30 P.M.	leisure time	
2:00 P.M.	language group	
2:30 P.M.	recess	
3:00 P.M.	music time	
3:15 P.M.	closing group	

Figure 3.2. Sample visual schedule for a student who functions at a high level of abstraction.

shape to other shapes. Words or information related to the central concept are written on the connecting lines or in the other shapes. As the map expands, the words become more specific and detailed. For students who are young or who require additional cues, semantic maps can use pictures for the key words or concepts. Figures 3.3 and 3.4 provide examples of semantic maps.

Analogy graphic organizers are another strategy for students with Asperger Syndrome. The teacher selects two concepts for which the students will begin to identify attributes. The

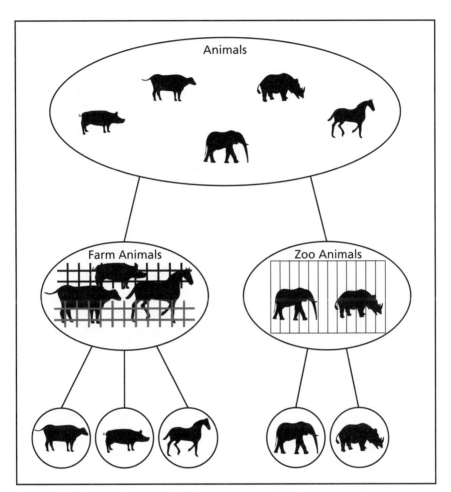

Figure 3.3. Semantic map with pictorial representation.

teacher and the students define how the two concepts are alike and how they differ, then draw a conclusion. Often the teacher has to assist students in identifying attributes by presenting choices, either written or pictorial, from which the students select. This task can be completed individually, in small groups, or as a class. Figures 3.5 and 3.6 provide examples of two commonly used analogy graphic organizers: the Venn diagram and the compare and contrast chart.

Outlines. Outlines are another visual support that can be effective for students with Asperger Syndrome. Because of motor and distraction and inattention problems, the student with Asperger

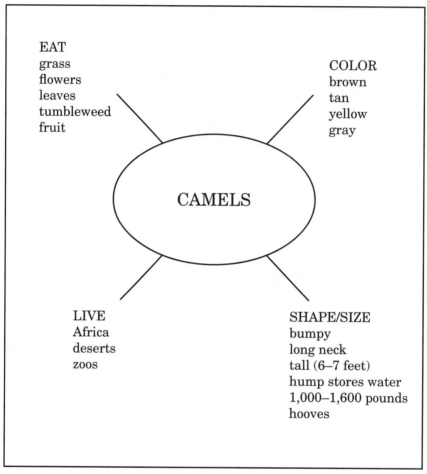

Figure 3.4. Semantic map.

Syndrome is often not good at taking notes on teacher lectures. Thus, teachers should help these students with note taking. The first step is to teach note taking. The student with Asperger Syndrome, as well as many other students, may neither understand the concept of main idea nor understand that a teacher's language cues students to salient information (i.e., when the teacher repeats an item or changes voice tone, the information is important). The teacher can assist the student by providing the following:

- *A complete outline.* This outline lists main points and details. It allows students to follow the lecture but frees them from taking notes.

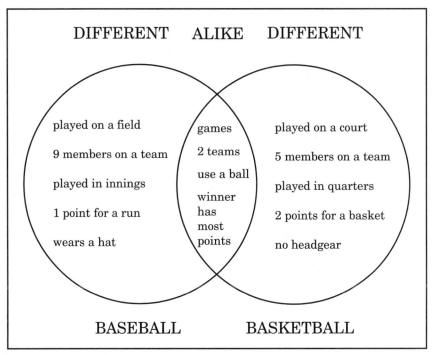

DIFFERENT   ALIKE   DIFFERENT

played on a field

9 members on a team

played in innings

1 point for a run

wears a hat

games

2 teams

use a ball

winner has most points

played on a court

5 members on a team

played in quarters

2 points for a basket

no headgear

BASEBALL   BASKETBALL

Figure 3.5. Venn diagram.

- *A skeletal outline.* This outline lists main points. Students may use this format to fill in pertinent details delivered through lectures.

- *Direct verbal cues.* Verbal cues, such as "This is the first main point" or "This detail should be included in your notes," assist students in knowing which points to include in their notes. At this stage, students may be responsible for taking complete notes. The verbal cues serve as prompts.

- *Subtle verbal cues.* Subtle verbal cues also provide clues regarding important information. Students need to recognize these cues, such as "The first branch of the federal government is the legislative branch. Did you write that in your notes?" or "You need to remember that the legislative branch makes the laws."

The note-taking level of students with Asperger Syndrome must be considered when selecting the appropriate type of

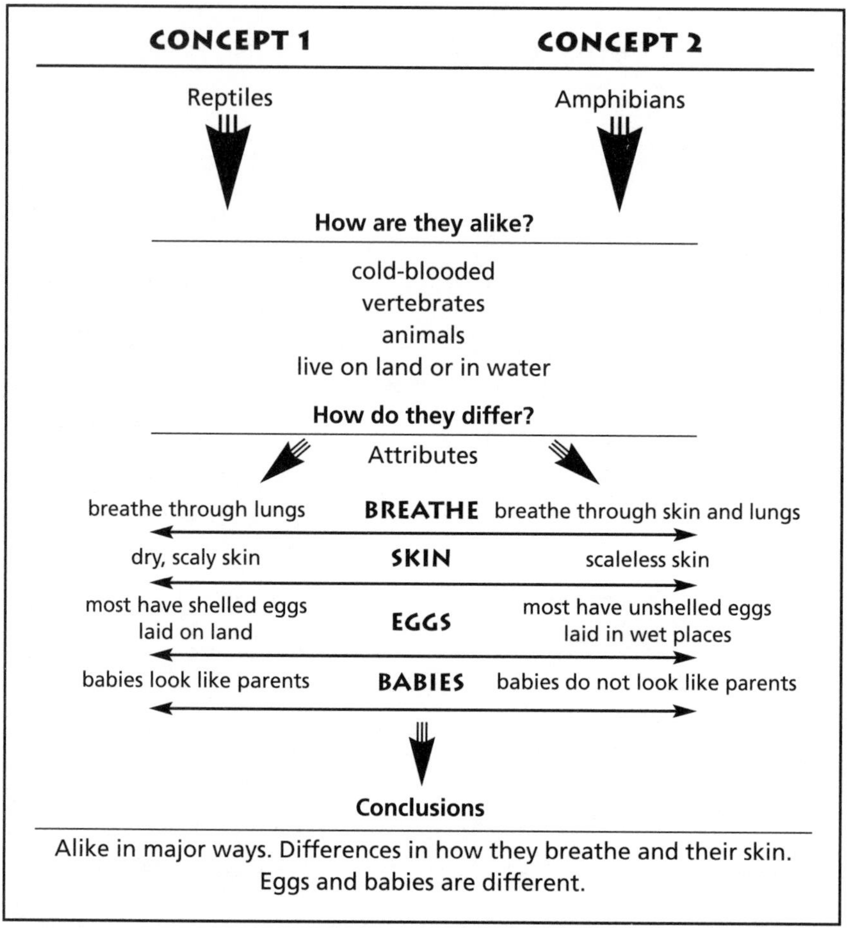

CONCEPT 1   CONCEPT 2

Reptiles   Amphibians

How are they alike?

cold-blooded
vertebrates
animals
live on land or in water

How do they differ?

Attributes

breathe through lungs	**BREATHE**	breathe through skin and lungs
dry, scaly skin	**SKIN**	scaleless skin
most have shelled eggs laid on land	**EGGS**	most have unshelled eggs laid in wet places
babies look like parents	**BABIES**	babies do not look like parents

Conclusions

Alike in major ways. Differences in how they breathe and their skin.
Eggs and babies are different.

Figure 3.6. Compare and contrast chart.

assistance. The types of assistance listed above can be considered hierarchical. When the student has mastered note taking at one level of assistance, the teacher can proceed to the next. Although they are hierarchical, the different types of assistance can be combined to facilitate the student's note taking. For example, a student with Asperger Syndrome may be able to work with a skeletal outline but require verbal cues to ensure that he identifies the important details. It is important to note, however, that all students will not proceed up this hierarchy. Some students may always require a complete or skeletal outline.

Other note-taking options include having a peer take notes using carbon paper, with the copy going to the student with Asperger Syndrome, or allowing the student who is adept with the computer to take notes using outlining software.

Task Cards. Task cards help individuals with Asperger Syndrome recall academic content, routines, or social skills. Typically presented on business-card-size paper, the task card sets out the steps the student must follow. Each statement on the card is a directive. The language on the task card is usually short and concise. For the adolescent, task cards can provide an overview of the routines and teacher expectations in each class. For younger children, a task card may outline four conversation starters that can be used with peers during lunch. For families taking vacations, a task card might outline the travel schedule (J. L. Savner, personal communication, February 2001). Figure 3.7 provides an example of a task card that reviews the daily routine in science class.

Preparation for Changes in Routine

Students with Asperger Syndrome are typically routine bound, and any schedule change can have deleterious effects on behavior. Thus, any major change in these students' schedules must be considered carefully. These students may need advance warning for fire drills, assemblies, pep rallies, or substitute teachers. Some students are so focused on routine that minor

---

SCIENCE

1. Go to locker.
2. Get green notebook, textbook, pencil, pen, and paper.
3. Go to class.
4. Exchange homework with lab partner and grade it using a pen.
5. Put graded homework in teacher's homework tray and wait for teacher instructions.
6. Do assigned work at the lab station with partner.

Figure 3.7. Sample task card. (This card should be about the size of a business card.)

changes cause behavioral problems. For example, the seriously routine-bound student may not be able to adapt easily to a change in the daily reading lesson. This student, who is accustomed to doing, say, a vocabulary exercise, oral reading, silent reading, and comprehension check, may lose control when the teacher varies the order of the activities or spends reading time playing a game of Jeopardy to test students' recall of the reading material.

Visual schedules that clearly outline what the student will be doing and what the expectations are for the new activity can help prepare the students for change. The teacher can write a one-time behavioral contract indicating the change, the tasks the student is responsible for completing, who will monitor the student, how the student will be monitored, and the reinforcement. The student and teacher review the document; after the teacher is certain that the student understands, both sign the document. The student can take the contract to the new situation and refer to it as necessary.

Buddy Program

A normally achieving peer who likes and understands the student with Asperger Syndrome can be an asset. Indeed, many parents have reported that a buddy or mentor has often made the difference in whether their children could cope with a school situation. Buddies can accompany these students during transitions, provide cues for appropriate behavior, and take notes for the students during class. In addition, buddies can provide the social interactions that many students with Asperger Syndrome desire but rarely succeed at unassisted.

Buddies must be carefully selected. They should be volunteers who understand the exceptionality, respect individual differences, and genuinely like the student. Typically, buddies should also be "model" students who are generally not susceptible to behaviors that parents and teachers would see as problematic (e.g., skipping school, acting disrespectfully toward adults and other students). Because students with Asperger Syndrome typically have poor social judgment, they might follow a peer into inappropriate social situations to have social interactions.

Early or Late Release

Transitions between classes or to special activities (e.g., music, physical education) are often extremely disruptive to students with Asperger Syndrome. Unanticipated schedule changes often cause these students to experience a high stress level, and when this is combined with unfavorable environmental conditions (e.g., students bumping into one another, the student feeling that she needs to rush, a feeling of uncertainty about where the activity is located, or taunting by peers), the student is likely to "fall apart." The student may have a meltdown or tantrum, and cry, "tune out," or refuse to comply. These behavioral problems often occur as a sort of self-protection. When the student is in a situation that he does not know how to handle, the student selects one of a limited number of coping strategies that is typically considered inappropriate by adults and peers.

These problems can be circumvented by providing the student with extra time to reach a destination. Releasing her 5 minutes before the bell rings or 5 minutes after the bell rings often effects a relatively stress-free environment (e.g., a hallway without many students, less noise) in which the student can get to a class, assembly, or other special event. This strategy may be particularly effective when combined with a transition buddy.

Assignment Notebooks

An effective organizational strategy for students with Asperger Syndrome is an assignment notebook if homework is given. All homework tasks and their due dates are listed in the notebook. Ideally, the assignment notebook also contains a sample of what the assignment should look like. The teacher monitors the assignment notebook to ensure that all assignments and all supporting materials (e.g., samples, texts, worksheets) are included. Parents work cooperatively with the teacher by reviewing the notebook nightly and signing it as the student completes tasks.

Timelines

Teachers often assign tasks, such as book reports and term papers, that must be completed over an extended period of time. Typically, teachers will announce the task, explain the steps necessary to complete the assignment, and set a due date. The expectation is that students will budget their time to complete the assignment by the due date. Most students work on the assignment piece by piece over days or weeks. However, because of a variety of difficulties (e.g., lack of ability to structure tasks over time, inability to project how long a task will take, general disorganization, failure to understand the complexity of the task), students with Asperger Syndrome will often try to write a 20-page term paper or read a 200-page book and write a report in 2 hours the evening before the assignment is due.

Teachers need to assist these students in budgeting their time. They should create a list of the steps needed to complete the task, help the student set target dates for completing each item, and establish a system to monitor the student over the course of the assignment. Monitoring should include asking to see the project at each stage because the student with Asperger Syndrome may indicate that a task is completed when in fact it is not. This untruth may not be deliberate; it may be a function of the disability. For example, if a teacher says to a student, "I hope you understand that you should have your book read by now," the student may respond affirmatively, indicating an understanding of the statement but not connecting the statement to any action that she should have taken. It is best for teachers to enlist the aid of parents in developing and monitoring timelines; however, in most cases the teacher should not trust the student to be the sole source of communication between home and school.

The Travel Card

The Travel Card uses a gridlike format that contains a brief list of the academic, behavior, and social strategies on which the student is working (Jones & Jones, 1995). These are typically listed as column heads. Down the side of the card, each of the student's classes is listed.

Students carry the Travel Card from class to class, and each teacher must sign the card and indicate, using a plus (+) or minus (–), whether the student is engaging in the targeted behaviors. The student's case manager or resource room teacher prepares the card and gives it to the student daily. The student then carries it to each class. The completed card is left with the student's last teacher, who returns it to the case manager. The student receives tokens for carrying the card as well as engaging in the targeted behavior. She charts and graphs her points weekly and selects a reinforcer from a menu of preferred items. The student may also choose to "bank" the points to save for reinforcers that require additional points.

Initially, the student may not be able to carry the card from class to class because of organizational problems. Several options exist for introducing the Travel Card system systematically. Initially, general education teachers may have to maintain the card, prompt the student to engage in the target behaviors, and ensure that the card is returned daily to the special educator. Alternatively, the Travel Card may be introduced in one setting, with other settings added as the student is successful. The ultimate goal is to have the student maintain responsibility for the card as well as prompt general education teachers to complete the Travel Card each hour.

The Travel Card increases students' productive behavior across multiple environments. It also facilitates teacher collaboration and improves school–home communication (Carpenter, 2001). Figure 3.8 is an example of a Travel Card.

Home Base

Students with Asperger Syndrome often view school as a stressful environment that presents several ongoing stressors of great magnitude, including difficulty predicting events because of changing schedules, tuning into and understanding teacher directions, and interacting with peers. Students with this exceptionality often fail to indicate in any meaningful way that they are under stress or experiencing difficulty coping. Quite often they just tune out, daydream, or state in a monotone voice a seemingly benign phrase such as "I don't know what to do." Because no emotion is conveyed, these behaviors often go unnoticed by teachers. Then at some point a student acts verbally or physically aggressive, seemingly without provocation. The student may scream or kick over a desk. This behavior seems to be unpredictable.

Some students with Asperger Syndrome do not display these types of behaviors in school. Sometimes teachers report that these students do fine in school, even with academic and social problems. However, parents report that when these children arrive home, they lose control. They have a tantrum, cry,

TRAVEL CARD

Date _____

Key: + = Yes   0 = No   NA = Not Applicable

	Did student follow teacher instructions?	Did student bring all materials?	Did student complete assignments?	Did student turn in homework?	Teacher's initials
Reading					
Science					
Geography					
Study Skills					
English					
Spanish					
Bonus Points	Went to nurse after getting off bus?			Has assignment book?	
Total	+ 0				

Teacher Comments/Suggestions/Announcements:

Figure 3.8. Sample Travel Card.

or are aggressive. It seems as if these students use all their self-control to manage at school, and once they get to a safe environment, they let go of some of the pressure they have bottled up inside.

What can educators do to help these students manage their stress at school and at home? In addition to instructing students on how to recognize and manage their stress levels, teachers can create a safe "home base" for students with Asperger Syndrome. This is a place where students can go when they feel the need to regain control. Resource rooms or counselors' offices can be safe places. When a student feels the need to leave the classroom, he or she can take assignments to the home base and work there in a less stressful environment. School personnel frequently schedule students' days so that they begin at the home base and then have frequent stops there. This allows students a teacher with whom they have a consistent relationship and a place to go when the need arises (Myles & Adreon, 2001; Myles & Southwick, 1999).

Instructional Sequence

Teachers must provide an instructional sequence that facilitates students' acquisition of information. This sequence includes effective lesson presentation and appropriate homework if the teacher decides to assign it.

Rationale

Students with Asperger Syndrome often need to understand how or why concepts required for mastery are relevant. Thus, teachers must tell the student (a) why the information is useful, (b) how the student can use it, and (c) where it fits in with the knowledge the student already possesses. As with students with other exceptionalities, students with Asperger Syndrome need to understand lesson rationale before they can or will learn.

Instruction

The teacher explains the goals for the content being presented and spells out exactly what the student needs to learn. Then, using a direct instructional format, the instructor teaches the content using visual and auditory stimuli. The teacher breaks down the information and presents it in small increments. This type of instruction is active, with the teacher presenting information, asking questions, and providing corrective feedback. In other words, direct instruction is not presenting a worksheet with a model and telling the student to follow the directions.

Modeling

During the modeling phase, the teacher gets the student's attention and shows the student what he or she is supposed to do. The instructor demonstrates how to complete a worksheet, participate in a cooperative group activity, begin a project, and so forth. It is important for the teacher to demonstrate how to correctly complete a task or assignment, instead of telling the student what not to do. Many students with Asperger Syndrome know what they should not do but have no understanding of what is required of them.

Models should be presented frequently. For some students with Asperger Syndrome, it may be necessary to present a model of how to put identifying information on a spelling test prior to each examination. The teacher should spell out every direction for these students, preferably with a visual component. The teacher cannot assume, for example, that a student knows to number his spelling paper to 20 just because he has always had 20 spelling words. Anything that is only implied by the teacher will likely not be understood by these students.

Interpretation

Throughout the lesson, the teacher must closely monitor the student's emotional state. Because students with Asperger Syndrome often have a flat, even seemingly negative affect, it is difficult to tell when they are stressed as a result of not comprehending specific content. The teacher must work with the student to understand how he or she communicates emotional distress and meet that student's needs through additional instruction, modeling, or individual work sessions. Failure to engage in this very important step can result in the student's tuning out or having a behavioral outburst.

Verification

Because of a propensity for tunnel vision and distraction and inattention, the student with Asperger Syndrome must be actively engaged throughout the instructional process. The student should be provided physical cues to attend to relevant stimuli and be asked frequent questions. Physical cues could come in the form of the teacher's staying close by and tapping briefly on the student's desk or using a prearranged signal (e.g., clearing the throat, placing a pencil on the student's desk, placing a hand on the student's shoulder).

For the student with Asperger Syndrome who requires a long processing time, the teacher might want to arrange a strategy so that the student knows when he or she will be asked a question. For example, the teacher might tell a student that she will be asked a question only when the teacher stands next to her. The teacher can then use this strategy, initially asking the student questions to which she knows the answers. No one else in the class needs to be aware that the student and teacher have this agreement.

A second strategy involves telling the student in advance what questions he or she will be asked during class. The questions could be presented in written format, oral format, or both, depending on the student's needs. The student will then be able to relax, process, and learn from the lecture without worrying about being unprepared to answer questions.

Verification also includes a generalization component. Teachers should work with students to ensure that they know the content and how to apply it across multiple settings and with multiple instructors.

Homework

Teachers and parents or caregivers should work together to determine whether homework should be assigned, and if so, how much. Because students with Asperger Syndrome have a marked need for structure, it is often best to assign tasks that can be completed at the home base or during a study hall.

If homework is assigned, it is best to use an assignment notebook and a parent–teacher communication system. This structure is necessary because parents or caregivers will play an active role in ensuring that the student completes assignments. Parents or caregivers need to set up a structure for assignment completion and monitoring similar to what the teachers use in school. In addition, they will most likely need to assist the student by clarifying and giving an overview of assignments. In some cases, a parent may need to model the task for the student. Thus, teachers should ensure that the parents or caregivers understand the homework. This is often difficult, because the teacher cannot simply send home a note to the parents—chances are it will never reach its destination. The disorganized student with Asperger Syndrome will misplace the note or bury it in the bottom of the backpack and forget that it is there.

To facilitate home–school communication, some schools have established a homework line that students and parents can call to hear an overview of assigned work. This sort of system is ideal for the student with Asperger Syndrome and his or her caregivers.

Motivation

Many students with Asperger Syndrome are difficult to motivate. They often see no reason to complete a task and frequently verbalize this to the teacher in a less than tactful, even blunt manner (e.g., "This makes no sense," "No one in the world does anything like this," "This is stupid"). These students are not intentionally being rude but merely stating what they consider to be a fact.

Following are some general ways to motivate the student with Asperger Syndrome.

- A rationale will often motivate the student to begin an assignment. However, if the student is one who likes to engage in verbal power struggles, giving a reason for completing an assignment may start a series of "Yes, but . . ." statements or reasons why the rationale is not relevant to the student.

- Another way to prompt the student to complete a task is to acknowledge the student's statement and then provide a global rule (e.g., "I know you think that no one does work like this, but everyone in this class . . .").

- Assignments that relate to student obsessions are often highly motivating if the obsession is a secondary one. In their desire to discuss, learn, and read about their particular interest, these students will often eagerly complete an assignment on the topic.

- A fourth way to motivate is to use the Premack principle, or "Grandma's Rule." The teacher can set a contingency on a visual schedule that says following completion of a nonpreferred task, the student can engage in a preferred activity.

- Often it is motivating for the student to complete an assignment with a peer. Because the motivation for social interaction is frequently strong, many students will complete nonpreferred tasks when they can work in pairs or small groups.

- If motivation is a problem, the teacher should determine whether student resistance is associated with motor skills. Owing to fine motor problems, the student often balks at an assignment, because the written portion is difficult. Providing a computer for assignment completion or allowing the student to dictate to a peer or into a tape recorder is often enough to prompt the student to begin a task. Some assignments can be modified from an essay to a multiple-choice format to further reduce written requirements. If the teacher is not testing handwriting, there is often little reason to require that an assignment be handwritten.

Teacher Interaction Strategies

Parents of students with Asperger Syndrome have often communicated that individual teachers have made a difference as to whether a particular student was successful in school. They have defined a variety of teacher characteristics that seem to match well these students' needs. Often these behaviors are not measurable but rather involve personality aspects. Overall, these teachers are consistent in the way they structure their classrooms and predictable in the way they act. They tend not to overrely on "top–down" management approaches, allowing the student options whenever possible. This type of teacher understands students with Asperger Syndrome, detecting their stress level and making accommodations as needed. Some additional effective teacher characteristics include the following:

- has a working knowledge of the characteristics of students with Asperger Syndrome

- develops a sense of trust between self and student

- accepts student's cognitive and social abilities and learning potential

- accepts the student as he or she is

- relates to the student's role in school
- enjoys working with the student and voices that enjoyment
- models enjoyment of doing tasks
- indicates that learning is mutual
- works as an unobtrusive facilitator rather than as a dictator
- reacts calmly to all students
- provides nonthreatening feedback
- does not lecture, but provides general direction as needed
- listens to the student, analyzes the student's needs, and adapts curriculum accordingly
- avoids asking "why" questions to understand behavior
- states expected behavior and provides examples
- uses short sentences
- limits the number of instructions that are given at one time
- provides instructions in more than one modality, realizing that visual memory is most often a strength for these students
- uses a matter-of-fact and unemotional tone to redirect the student
- states rules as universals ("Everyone in this class needs to listen when I talk")
- behaves in a predictable and dependable manner
- provides adequate wait time for the student to process instructions
- provides a classroom structure that is predictable

Concluding Thoughts

Students with Asperger Syndrome, because of their intellectual capabilities, have the potential to be successful in school settings. However, intellectual functioning alone is not enough to ensure that these students have the structure and support they need. Educators must develop environmental modifications and teach strategic skills that these students can use throughout their academic day. Visual, structural, and motivational strategies are integral to these students' success. Just as important to their success is selection of a teacher whose characteristics match their needs. Supports must be set into place with careful consideration of how these students' needs can best be met.

Planning for Behavioral Success

4

Children and adolescents with Asperger Syndrome are particularly prone to social peculiarities, social interaction difficulties, behavioral problems, and, to a lesser degree, aggression. Although they are frequently motivated to be near to and to socially engage peers and adults, children and youth with Asperger Syndrome are deficient in age-appropriate, reciprocal social interaction skills such as those required to participate in cooperative play and related activities. These children and youth are often described by others as socially stiff and awkward, emotionally flat, socially unaware, self-absorbed, lacking in empathy, prone to show socially unacceptable behavior, and insensitive or unaware of verbal and nonverbal social cues. Indeed, virtually every educational characteristic of students with Asperger Syndrome is related to their behavior and social skills. Accordingly, professionals and families must provide specialized support so that these children and adolescents can progress and experience success at school and at home. This chapter presents behavior management options available to professionals and families.

Social and Behavioral Assessment

The basic model for assessing children and youth with Asperger Syndrome consists of the same general effective-practice elements as for other individuals, with or without disabilities: (a) Identify and measure at least one behavior to change; (b) analyze the functions of target behaviors and related environmental and antecedent factors; and (c) select, implement, and evaluate appropriate interventions and treatments. Each of these components is discussed here as it relates to children and youth with Asperger Syndrome.

Identifying and Measuring Behavior To Change

Identifying and measuring behaviors that need to be modified requires specifying those target behaviors. Behaviors such as "nonreciprocal social responding," "auditory hypersensitivity," and "sensory and emotional overload" mean different things to different people and therefore are unsuitable as targets for behavioral intervention programs. Instead, target behaviors need to be specified so that they reflect exactly what the behavior is (e.g., one should not say that a child has a problem with auditory hypersensitivity, but rather should identify the target behavior as "loud screaming"). Where and when the behaviors occur is also specified (e.g., loud screaming in any classroom or indoor setting during regular school hours). Such specificity helps adults involved in change programs understand and evaluate interventions. It also enables children with Asperger Syndrome to be knowledgeable and involved participants in program efforts on their behalf.

Behavior data should be regularly and accurately measured before an intervention is implemented. Such measurement continues after a strategy is implemented. Measurement options most appropriate for children and youth with Asperger Syndrome include frequency counts (the number of times a particular behavior is observed), duration assessment (the length of time a behavior lasts), and interval and time sampling. Interval and time sampling involve dividing an observation period into equal time segments and observing whether the target behavior occurs within each segment. Interval sampling requires observation during an entire time segment (e.g., 30 seconds), whereas time sampling requires brief observation of a target response at the end of each segment (e.g., the observer notes whether the child is engaged in a particular behavior at the end of each 30-second segment).

Depending on the nature of the targeted behavior and on resource availability, the appropriate measurement procedure is selected. For example, if the target behavior is tantrums, a duration assessment is selected instead of frequency counts, because the length of time a child throws a tantrum is usually more informative than the number of times he throws a tantrum. Similarly, if the goal of an intervention program is to reduce the number of times a child is out of her assigned seat during a particular class, frequency counts would likely be most suitable.

Analyzing Functions of Target Behaviors and Related Factors

The functions of target behaviors and related factors are analyzed in an attempt to answer two questions: What is motivating the targeted behavior? and What are the conditions that are most and least apt to be present when the behavior occurs? For instance, does a child engage in an undesired social behavior as a way of getting peer attention because he lacks more appropriate ways of meeting his need for recognition? Is the behavior more likely to occur at certain times, in the presence of certain people, or in certain settings or environments? Is a target behavior most apt to occur while a student is working on certain types of assignments? Knowing the motivation for a behavior or that a behavior is correlated with particular factors is of obvious assistance in developing an appropriate intervention program. For example, determining that a child primarily engages in argumentative behavior with one paraeducator, as opposed to all teachers and staff, suggests possible causes for the behavior and thus helps in the creation of an intervention program that will have the highest probability of positively influencing the target behavior.

This process of identifying environmental and other antecedents of particular behaviors, along with motivators for those behaviors, is known as a *functional assessment*. In this context, an *antecedent* is any variable that precedes a target behavior, such as the time of day when particular social problems arise, the instructions given by a teacher prior to a student's displaying a problem behavior, and so forth. A related term in this process is *functional analysis*. A functional analysis is a more specific process wherein the persons conducting the assessment systematically evaluate function and antecedent hypotheses about the target behaviors. Based on an understanding of these variables, suitable intervention programs can be developed. Because children and youth with Asperger Syndrome frequently display behaviors that are difficult to understand, functional assessment and functional analysis information is essential. Indeed, it is extremely difficult to craft effective behavior management programs for learners with Asperger Syndrome without such information.

There are two major general assumptions associated with conducting a functional analysis or assessment. First, it is assumed that the behavior of children and youth with Asperger Syndrome, as is the case with all human behavior, serves a purpose. Accordingly, professionals and families who evaluate the behavior and social interactions of individuals with Asperger Syndrome must assume that these responses, regardless of how apparently nonfunctional they may appear, have a purpose. Thus, these responses satisfy some need or are designed to achieve some goal, such as communication, escaping an undesired task, and so forth, even if form (i.e., how the child communicates) and function (i.e., why the child communicates) appear to be unrelated.

The second assumption associated with functional analysis or assessment is that behaviors are controlled by, or are connected with, antecedent and other environmental factors. Consequences of behaviors are the responses they evoke from others. For example, a child's inappropriate social initiations with peers might routinely have as a response consequence verbal reprimands from adults.

Functional analyses are based on indirect and direct procedures. Indirect methods include review and analysis of student records and files; interviews of professionals such as teachers and physicians, parents, and the students themselves regarding specified behavioral and social interaction patterns; and functional assessment scales and questionnaires. In contrast, direct functional analysis methods and procedures rely on direct observations and direct testing of antecedent and consequent variables thought to be associated with particular responses. Specific direct functional analysis methods include ABC analysis (where A = antecedent, B = behavior, C = consequence) and scatterplots.

Indirect Functional Assessment Methods

A primary initial source for understanding the antecedents and motivators associated with a student's behavior is his or her records and files. As shown in Table 4.1, varied sources of information are almost always available to help professionals and families understand children and their behavior. For example, a student's file may reflect that noisy settings such as crowded lunchrooms and gyms are apt to be upsetting to the student and may even provoke tantrums, or that a change of classroom personnel (e.g., a substitute teacher) may be associated with social withdrawal. Analysis of such records independent of other information and data is rarely sufficient to complete an appropriate functional assessment or analysis. However, these data and information form a foundation for understanding the child and the child's behavior and serve to direct subsequent functional assessment and analysis steps.

Another source of indirect functional assessment information is interviews of professionals, parents, and students. Indeed, informant assessment relies heavily on use of interviews with educators and other professionals and with parents and family members. Furthermore, whenever possible, the student with Asperger Syndrome should also be included in these interviews. Information generated through these interviews provides additional background and understanding of antecedents and motivators associated with the student's social interactions and behaviors. Moreover, these sessions provide a means of comparing responses across individuals. For example, knowing that a child's aggressive behaviors are shown only in the presence of certain teachers or family members would be extremely helpful in planning an appropriate management and social interaction

Table 4.1
Record Review Information Examples

Medical/ Physical	Social History	Response to Environment	Classroom and Educational
Growth and development history	Family SES	Response to environmental changes	Peer interactions
	Parent occupation		Preferred activities
Vision and hearing	Siblings	Response to: noise	Educational setting
			Grades
Medications	Custody arrangements	various foods lights	IEPs
Allergies		crowds	Response to rules
Health records	Family supports	temperatures demands	Behavior problems
Illnesses		peers	Response to task difficulty
			Response to time demands

enhancement program. The interview form shown in Figure 4.1 offers an example for obtaining information regarding the antecedent conditions surrounding a target behavior.

Scales and questionnaires are a third source of indirect functional assessment and functional analysis information. These instruments are designed to identify possible antecedent variables and motivators associated with target behaviors. These instruments vary in quality, with some offering excellent background information and data. For example, Lewis, Scott, and Sugai (1994) provided a simple questionnaire designed to elicit information about specific behavior problems. Based on a "typical episode of a problem behavior," the instrument is used to assess the percentage of time (i.e., ranging from *never* to *always*) each of 15 statements is perceived to be true for a particular student (e.g., "Does the problem behavior occur during specific academic activities?"). The instrument allows individuals conducting a functional assessment to generate information and develop hypotheses related to antecedent variables and peers' and adults' perceptions of escape and attention functions. A similarly designed scale, the *Motivation Assessment Scale* (Durand & Crimmins, 1992), provides professionals information needed to conduct an evaluation of four possible functions served by the behavior: sensory, escape, attention, and tangible.

Direct Functional Analysis Methods

In contrast to indirect functional assessment, direct functional analysis involves directly observing students to analyze their behaviors. The first step in conducting a direct functional analysis involves operationally defining and measuring a target behavior. That is, a desired social interaction behavior or other socially valid target behavior is clearly defined by identifying its salient elements. For example, a desired social interaction behavior such as playing appropriately with other children might be defined as follows: When on the playground at recess, Walter will approach a peer from his classroom and engage in an appropriate cooperative behavior (e.g., play tetherball, jump rope, tag) for at least 5 continuous minutes.

Step 2 of the direct functional analysis involves observing and describing the antecedents and consequences that are associated with the behavior's occurrence and nonoccurrence. Two

Name of individual being observed _____

Observer _____

Target behavior observational definition _____

_____

_____

Timing of target behavior

Target behavior primarily occurs

☐ during structured activities
  Explain: _____

☐ during unstructured activities
  Explain: _____

☐ during lecture times or times of group discussion
  Explain: _____

☐ when working or playing with others
  Explain: _____

☐ when working or playing alone
  Explain: _____

☐ during free time
  Explain: _____

☐ during times of transition
  Explain: _____

☐ primarily during morning hours
  Explain: _____

☐ primarily during afternoon hours
  Explain: _____

☐ in specific environments (e.g., classroom, lunchroom, gym)
  Explain: _____

☐ other
  Explain: _____

Relation of target behavior to the presence of others

Target behavior primarily occurs

☐ when working or playing with another student at school
  ☐ specific peer
  ☐ all peers
  Explain: _____

(continues)

Figure 4.1. Environmental and antecedent analysis form.

☐ when working or playing with a sibling or peer at home or in the
  community
  ☐ specific siblings
  ☐ all siblings
  ☐ specific peer
  ☐ all peers
  Explain: _____

☐ when working or interacting with an adult at school
  ☐ specific adult
  ☐ all adults
  Explain: _____

☐ when working or interacting with a parent or other adult at home
  or in the community
  ☐ specific parent
  ☐ both parents
  ☐ specific adult
  ☐ all adults
  Explain _____

☐ while a student is working on certain types of assignments
  Explain: _____

Summary analysis of timing of target behavior, presence of others, and other correlates of target behavior.

_____
_____
_____
_____
_____
_____

Figure 4.1. *Continued.*

ways of conducting such analyses are to use ABC charts and scatterplots.

• *ABC charts.* ABC charts offer a structured means of observing and analyzing the antecedents (A), consequences (C), and responses (R) of children to the consequences of adults and peers associated with a target behavior (B). For example, an ABC analysis might focus on a child's demonstrating appropriate social behavior in a cooperative group activity with peers. In this scenario, targeting "appropriate social behavior" (B), the A (antecedent) parts of the analysis would include the classroom setting, teachers and children the child was with, time of day, curriculum and classroom activities, the specific instructions and prompts the student was presented, and so forth. The C (consequences) element of the analysis would involve analyzing the reactions or responses of the target child's teachers and peers when he did and did not demonstrate appropriate cooperative group behavior. Finally, the child's responses (R) to these teacher and peer consequences of his behavior would be analyzed. For example, the student's appearing to be pleased by the attention he received from peers for appropriate social behavior would be important information to have in forming hypotheses and developing and implementing an effective intervention program.

For example, a 16-year-old with Asperger Syndrome routinely begins crying and screaming in the hallway during class breaks. During these periods (four 5-minute breaks), the school psychologist makes the observations shown in Figure 4.2. The psychologist has determined that the student routinely goes into the hallway outside his classroom during class breaks and begins asking other students if they are aware of various school rules. This student is well versed in the rules and in fact always carries a copy of the school's disciplinary code. He reminds students that it is against school rules to smoke on school property, and security personnel will be called if somebody is observed smoking. In response to these reminders, his peers have begun intimating that it is acceptable to engage in behaviors identified as unacceptable in the school handbook (e.g., students are allowed to smoke on school property). Confronted with this contradiction, the student with Asperger Syndrome tries to show his peers the written rule, but they indicate that they will call security personnel to "arrest" the student. The student consequently becomes upset and starts crying and screaming, much to the delight of his peers. Prompted by the crying and screaming, teachers or administrators attempt to calm or discipline the student.

Use of a functional analysis method such as the one shown in Figure 4.2 does not guarantee an effective intervention program. However, a functional analysis is an efficient and effective tool for understanding variables and outcomes related to students' problems, and for designing and implementing appropriate intervention programs.

• *Scatterplots.* Scatterplots are used to help identify contextual conditions associated with target responses; that is, they are used to

Time	Setting	Task	Behavior (B), consequence (C), and response (R) analysis
8:55–9:00	hallway outside class (class break)	none	B: Target student approaches group of students to remind them of school rules. Begins reading various school rules and consequences for infractions.
			C: Peers ignore student; one peer tells student to go away.
			R: Target student retreats and reads class rule book.
			B: Target student repeats rules; reminds peers that security personnel may be called to enforce rules.
			C: Peer informs student that rules don't apply to them: "Mr. Walker [principal] says it's okay to smoke in school."
			R: Target student attempts to show peer the written rule. When peer refuses to look at the rule book and indicates that security personnel are being sent, student begins to cry and scream and continues until quieted by a teacher assigned to patrol hallways.

Figure 4.2. Functional analysis observation example.

understand a target behavior relative to time, setting, activity, personnel, and so forth. For example, a child might be observed for classroom talk-outs and subsequent removal from class to determine if particular parts of her curriculum are more highly correlated with the target response than others.

Step 3 in the direct functional analysis involves analyzing direct and indirect functional analysis data for possible antecedents and consequences and forming hypotheses to explain the target behavior. For example, in the case shown in Figure 4.2, teachers and staff might hypothesize that the student's peculiar social interactions relating to school rules is associated with one or more of the following: need for peer attention, failure to understand conventional peer interaction protocol, or communication based exclusively on a narrowly defined obsessive interest.

Following identification of possible hypotheses related to a target behavior, Step 4 in the direct functional analysis is testing the hypotheses. Testing involves systematically observing an individual's target behavior under various antecedent and consequent conditions. For example, in the Figure 4.2 case, the teachers and staff might decide that the student's problem behavior is likely a function of his desire for peer attention in combination with his failure to understand conventional peer interaction protocol. By systematically providing the student more appropriate ways of gaining peer attention and alternative topics for peer discussion, they could likely determine whether or not the hypothesized reasons were responsible for the target behavior. This diagnostic determination would then be used to develop an appropriate intervention program.

Strategies for Behavioral Success

As previously outlined, the steps leading to selection, implementation, and evaluation of an appropriate intervention for an individual with Asperger Syndrome are preliminary, albeit indispensable, steps. That is, it is unlikely that intervention will succeed without a clearly defined and measured target behavior; a thorough analysis of salient antecedent variables (e.g., curriculum or activity most associated with a target behavior, personnel connected to a problem, environments most likely to be associated with a target response, time of day when a targeted behavior is most and least apt to occur); and an understanding of functions that motivate a particular response (e.g., attention, failure to understand, communication, avoidance of an undesired activity). At the same time, the aforementioned information does not always easily reveal a clear and unitary intervention. For instance, knowing that a child's out-of-seat classroom behavior typically occurs in math class, during independent written work time, and that it is likely motivated by an attempt to escape the activity does not automatically tell an intervention team the most effective and efficient strategy to use. Thus, in the present example an intervention might involve one or more of the following strategies: modification of the task, including its level of difficulty, length, and so forth; social prompts and reinforcement for completing the task; use of a peer to prompt the student to work on the assigned task and to give the student social support; use of a self-monitoring or self-reinforcement program; and use of a number of other options. Indeed, selection of an appropriate intervention strategy involves consideration of a variety of options that fit a particular student and the circumstances. Children and youth with Asperger Syndrome tend to be highly individualized in their responses, preferences, and tolerance for various strategies. Accordingly, there is no reliable formula that can be used to specify an exact intervention or support plan. However, in spite of the availability of a reliable generic intervention formula, parents and professionals are nonetheless able to craft appropriate support programs based on preintervention information and data in combination with consideration of the unique characteristics of individual students.

Because of the unique and individual characteristics of students with Asperger Syndrome, intervention teams are advised to consider using a variety of effective practice methods. These methods may be categorized under the following headings: (a) environmental structuring and support methods and (b) behavioral interventions. Because individuals with Asperger Syndrome have a propensity for meltdowns when under stress, procedures for coping with such problems are also advised.

Structuring the Environment for Behavioral Success

It is clear that children and youth with Asperger Syndrome do not learn social behaviors in the same fashion as their nondisabled peers. That is, they do not spontaneously and incidentally learn myriad and highly complex social responses, almost all of which vary at least slightly from situation to situation. For instance, beginning at a young age, children are expected to discriminate among situations in which it is appropriate to talk to and interact with other children (e.g., during recess as opposed to classroom "quiet time") and to select conversational topics that correspond to various situations, circumstances, and shared interests. Thus, a child waiting in line with peers for her turn in a game of kickball is more likely to experience a positive peer response to a conversation about the ball game or similar activity than to a conversation about an unrelated, narrowly defined topic in which other students have little or no interest.

Without assistance, most children and youth with Asperger Syndrome will display a variety of socially incorrect, unaccepted, and nonreciprocal behaviors. Moreover, without support these individuals are vulnerable to emotional stress and apt to become agitated by social situations that they misinterpret. Structure for children with Asperger Syndrome also minimizes their being teased, bullied, or taken advantage of by peers.

There are no universally effective methods for structuring environments and situations for children with Asperger Syndrome. Nevertheless, these children generally benefit from predictable environments. The security that comes from being able to anticipate and understand activities, schedules, and expectations helps these children remain calm and enables them to appropriately meet various classroom, home, and community demands. Procedures that are helpful in creating such structure include (a) establishing clear expectations and rules for social behavior; (b) creating routines and schedules; and (c) offering physical, environmental, cognitive, and attitudinal support.

Expectations and Rules

Use of clear expectations for social and behavioral performance is one of the more effective and efficient means of establishing structure for children with Asperger Syndrome. The importance of such expectations to these children's behavioral and social success is obvious: Children and youth with Asperger Syndrome routinely experience difficulty understanding expectations and consequences. Accordingly, adults involved with these children must clearly and explicitly state, model, and illustrate rules, including desired behaviors; that is, children with Asperger Syndrome should be instructed not only in what not to do but also in acceptable behaviors. For example, students should not be told only that they are not permitted to play in the unfenced area next to the school where the teachers' cars are parked; rather, they should be instructed that they are permitted to play in the paved, fenced area around the school. Without such specificity, it cannot be assumed that children with Asperger Syndrome will understand and be able to follow rules.

Rules established for these children should also be utilitarian. Although this suggestion has obvious relevance for all children, it appears to be particularly important for children and youth with Asperger Syndrome. *Rule-related functional value* refers to establishing and enforcing rules that clearly and deliberately reinforce and facilitate students' social and cognitive development. For instance, adults should not establish rules that are designed merely to develop children's compliance or establish that the adults are "in charge" and otherwise have no functional value.

Also, rules and expectations should be regularly reviewed, and children should practice following rules by rehearsing desired classroom, home, and community behaviors and simulating potentially problematic situations. Finally, adults should closely monitor rules, maintain consistent expectations, and consistently apply consequences.

Expectations for behavior in the classroom and at home can be clarified by incorporating reviews of the expectations into daily routines. For example, an adult might briefly review playground rules prior to recess or grocery store behavior prior to entering the store. Classroom and school rules and expectations should be presented visually, for example, on bulletin board posters that identify appropriate rules for an activity, as in the following:

▶ **During Free Reading Time**

> Choose a book or magazine to read.
> You may read anywhere in the room.
> You may read with a friend.
> You must read quietly.
> When the timer goes off, quietly return to your desk.

Expectations and rules may also be visually communicated without use of written words. In this context, Figure 4.3 illustrates a visually formatted method of structuring leisure-time choices for a youth who experienced difficulty choosing and staying with appropriate tasks during earned free time. The student was required to choose from the leisure-time options shown, and to remain engaged in the activity he selected for a minimum of 10 minutes.

Figure 4.3. Example of visually structured leisure-time choices.

Another means of helping children understand and follow rules is for adults to identify cues or use physical prompts that alert students that their behavior is unacceptable. For example, a teacher may indicate that he will hold up a clipboard when he observes a child failing to take her turn in a game during recess. In this scenario, the student would rehearse coming to the teacher for instruction on appropriate play behavior whenever she observed her teacher holding a clipboard above his head.

Routines and Schedules

Routines and schedules can also provide structure for children and youth with Asperger Syndrome, building on their preference for predictability, order, and consistency. Most children and youth who are not disabled are able to effectively respond to environmental variables and to adapt to their everchanging world.

In contrast, children and youth with Asperger Syndrome tend to focus on only certain environmental variables and to have strong negative reactions to environmental changes. For example, a youth may fail to respond to information heard over the school intercom system. Other children with Asperger Syndrome may become extremely upset when classroom schedules are adjusted to accommodate a schoolwide assembly or to respond to inclement weather.

Even though resistance to change is a common characteristic of individuals with Asperger Syndrome, it is neither possible nor desirable to follow a routine without deviation. Nonetheless, it is important to recognize that many individuals with Asperger Syndrome have a strong preference for routine and consistency. Thus, teachers, families, and others who are in regular contact with these children would be wise to establish and follow predictable routines and to prepare the children in advance of anticipated changes. For example, after discussing the situation, a parent may follow an alternate route to school. Although such a deviation may seem trivial, it may be significant for a child with Asperger Syndrome.

It is important to build on preferences for routine and consistency while introducing strategies to help children deal with change, because learning to adjust to change has obvious implications for the well-being and development of individuals with Asperger Syndrome. Group and individual schedules presented in written, pictorial, or combination format, as shown in Figures 4.4 and 4.5, are useful in communicating the sequence of daily activities and in alerting children to new activities and schedule deviations.

Physical, Environmental, Cognitive, and Attitudinal Support

Physical, environmental, cognitive, and attitudinal support involves having adequate resources to effectively sustain, manage, and supervise children and youth with Asperger Syndrome in various settings, including classrooms and other school settings such as play areas and lunchrooms; home settings; and community settings such as shopping centers, churches, and recreational sites.

Above and beyond all other resources, it is essential that children and youth with Asperger Syndrome associate with adults

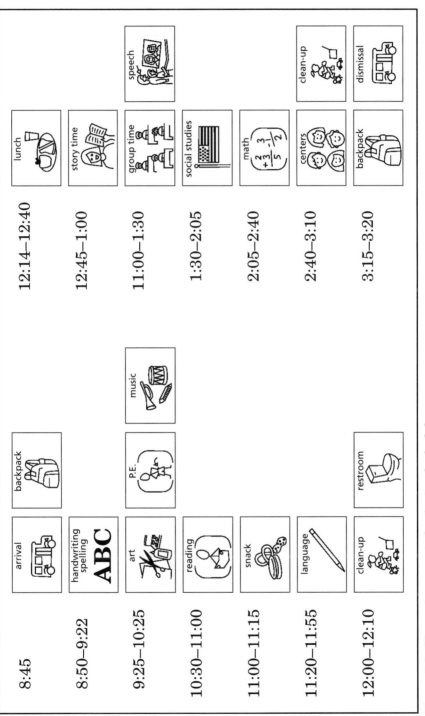

Figure 4.4. Elementary-age student's visual schedule.

THURSDAY, NOVEMBER 1		
Classes	**Room Number**	**Targets**
Homeroom	8	Check to-do list assignment
Math	9	Write homework
Language Arts	10	Bring keyboard and journal
P.E.	11	Hang with peer support guys
Lunch	12	Sit with Mac—use social scripts for conversation
Science	1	Check contract for focusing
History	2	Write homework
Resource Room	3	Check with Ms. Taylor re: point system feedback
Computer Club	4	Have fun!

Figure 4.5. Secondary-age student's written schedule.

and peers who are knowledgeable about the disorder, aware of individual needs, and capable of creating environments and situations to support these needs. It is essential that children with Asperger Syndrome have the support of parents, family members, peers, teachers, and other support personnel (e.g., psychologists, speech–language pathologists, paraprofessionals) who are knowledgeable and skilled in understanding and working with persons with Asperger Syndrome. In far too many instances, peers have bullied and provoked children with Asperger Syndrome into engaging in inappropriate behaviors out of ignorance and have otherwise exploited their social disability. Accordingly, one major step in preparing supportive environments for these children is to inform peers and teachers of the nature of the disorder, explain their role in supporting the children, and enlist their help in ensuring appropriate protection of these individuals.

Behavioral Interventions

Support for children and youth with Asperger Syndrome can also come in the form of behavioral interventions that are compatible with these children's unique social characteristics. In this context, behavioral interventions refer to (a) manipulation of antecedent conditions (variables that precede a target behavior), such as changing a student's assignment to reduce stress and to prevent a problem from occurring; and (b) use of positive and negative consequences (stimuli presented contingent upon a particular response, such as social praise for desired behavior). The uniqueness of children and youth with Asperger Syndrome warrants particular attention when behavioral interventions are being considered. These children require behavioral intervention strategies that do not rely heavily on a typical top–down approach. Strategies that work best with this population include those in which students have an interest, investment, and choice. Accordingly, it is strongly recommended that children with Asperger Syndrome be involved in program development and implementation. Such participation increases their understanding of rules, expectations, and consequences and increases the chance that they will be proactive in program implementation and evaluation.

Cognitive Behavior Modification

Cognitive behavior modification is a technique that teaches individuals to monitor their own behavior, pace, or performance and to deliver self-reinforcement at established intervals. In this strategy, the locus of behavior control is shifted from an external source, such as a teacher or supervisor, to the individual. Cognitive behavior modification can be used to facilitate a variety of behavior changes, from task completion to on-task behavior in either school or work settings. The procedure is most appropriate for students who have the necessary skills to independently perform a particular task but are unable to complete it because of attention difficulties. It is usually not appropriate for the student who does not possess the skills necessary to complete assigned work. The six steps required for implementing cognitive behavior modification are detailed in Table 4.2.

Reinforcers

Related to use of behaviorally based management programs, reinforcers refer to interventions that increase the occurrence of a

(*text continues on page 114*)

Table 4.2

Steps for Implementing a Cognitive
Behavior Modification Program

---

1. Pretraining Preparation

TARGET THE PROBLEM AREA. The first step in implementing a cognitive behavior modification (CBM) training program is to identify the problem behavior. It is recommended that only one behavior be targeted at any one time. Target behaviors typically fall into three classes: (a) behaviors that need to be decreased (i.e., those that are disruptive, distracting, or dangerous to self or others), (b) behaviors that need to be increased (i.e., those the student performs 60% to 80% of the time with teacher assistance), and (c) behaviors that need to be maintained (i.e., those the student performs at least 80% of the time without teacher assistance). One of the most important goals is to target a behavior that a person exhibits on some level and increase either the frequency or quality of the behavior.

The student should actively participate in targeting a behavior for change. The teacher and student should jointly discuss and define the inappropriate and appropriate behaviors. However, the teacher should first have a general idea of the behavior to be changed. In addition, the teacher should be prepared to define the behavior so that it is meaningful to the student.

IDENTIFY REINFORCERS. The CBM strategy is usually more successful if student preferences for reinforcers are used. The teacher must decide which types of reinforcement will accompany CBM, the frequency with which the reinforcement will occur, and how it will be faded. Although three types of reinforcement can be used (social, contingent activities, tangible/edible), teachers should emphasize the use of higher level reinforcers, particularly those that are social in nature.

PREPARE MATERIALS. Three items must be prepared: a timing device, a data collection sheet, and self-management tools. The creation, organization, and use of the materials should be practical so that they will be easy to use for both the student and the teacher. Materials should also be selected based on student preference.

Timing devices such as an audiotape or wristwatch can be used to designate time intervals. The length of the intervals should be commensurate with student attention to task. A timing signal will cue the student that it is time to document behavior. For example, if a student can stay on task for approximately 10 minutes, the signal should occur at 10-minute intervals. The student may require instruction on how to use the timing device.

A data collection sheet is used to monitor student progress and to determine strategy effectiveness. The type of data collection sheet used depends on the type of data collected. For example, frequency data allow teachers to measure the number of intervals the student was on task. Duration data can be used to measure the amount of time in minutes that a behavior occurs. The

(continues)

Table 4.2

Steps for Implementing a Cognitive
Behavior Modification Program *Continued.*

1. **Pretraining Preparation** *Continued.*

teacher may elect to synthesize student progress on a graph. This provides
a visual representation of the student's progress based on the data collected.
The student might also keep a bar graph showing on-task behavior.

The type of self-management tool is dependent on the student's functioning level and the task. The student may use a self-monitoring sheet
that resembles other seatwork materials to record on-task behavior. The
teacher and student should clearly design materials and discuss their
use so that they can be consistently and accurately used.

2. **Discrimination Training**

The discrimination training component assists students in becoming
aware of their own behavior and how it affects learning and successful
task completion. During this stage, the student is taught to distinguish
appropriate and inappropriate behavior, as well as incomplete and complete tasks. Instructional methods for use during discrimination training include: videotaping, picture cues, direct teaching, modeling, verbal
feedback, and physical guidance through the task. Because many students with Asperger Syndrome are not aware of how their behaviors
affect task completion, it is important to provide them with a concrete
representation.

Videotaping the student during the same classroom period that the CBM
strategy will be used is an effective way to promote self-awareness. A 15-
minute sample of seatwork behavior is generally sufficient for use during
the discrimination training session. If data are being collected to document behavior change, a minimum of 5 days of videotape should be taken.
This serves as baseline data. The videotape helps the student realize relationships, such as that between off-task behavior and failure to complete
assigned work. The student is presented with concrete evidence of off-task
behavior, thereby helping the student gain a clear perception of actual behavior without allowing denial mechanisms to cloud the issue. However,
care should be taken to prevent this step from being viewed as punitive.
The positive aspects of on-task behavior should be emphasized.

The teacher then introduces CBM, explaining that this strategy will help
the student increase on-task behavior and task completion. The teacher
and student view the videotape of student performance, discussing the
student's feelings about behaviors seen on the tape. The student then
identifies three specific on-task and three specific off-task behaviors seen
on the tape and records them on a seatwork behavior chart. Finally, the
teacher and the student work together to define a specific criterion for

(continues)

Table 4.2
Steps for Implementing a Cognitive
Behavior Modification Program *Continued.*

2. Discrimination Training *Continued.*

target behavior occurrence. Often, students with Asperger Syndrome initially suggest that they be held to 100% accuracy for all sessions. However, this is not realistic for most tasks. The teacher should guide the student to select a reasonable criterion. The student may be directed to observe the behavior of another student to develop this goal.

3. Self-Management Implementation

During self-management implementation, the teacher explains the CBM strategy. The student will learn through receiving a rationale, as well as through direct instruction, modeling, and guided practice. Self-management implementation depends on the method used, as well as on the student and his or her abilities, because each person learns at a different rate. Thus, what may take one person a few weeks to master may take another person a month.

The teacher instructs the student on the following steps:

a. *Self-monitoring.* The student listens to the timing signal. When the student hears the signal, he or she will question, "Am I paying attention?"

b. *Self-recording.* The student quickly assesses whether he or she was attending. If the student was attending, he or she will circle "yes" on the self-monitoring sheet. If the student was off task, he or she will circle "no" on the self-monitoring sheet.

c. *Self-rewarding.* The student rewards himself or herself for on-task behavior by saying, "Good job." If the student was off task, he or she will silently prompt, "Get back to work." The student resumes work immediately.

The teacher models these three steps using the videotape that was prepared earlier. The teacher views the videotape with the student and models the self-monitoring process by listening for the timing signal, stopping the videotape when it is heard, and asking, "Is (student's name) paying attention?" The teacher then verbalizes the answer and marks the appropriate answer on the self-monitoring sheet. Finally, the teacher models the use of the reward or prompting statement.

After the teacher has modeled the strategy for several minutes, the student attempts to self-monitor while viewing the videotape. Initially, it will be necessary for the teacher to direct the process and give assistance to the student. During this step of the training, it is important that the student use overt speech, that is, vocalize the self-assessment, reward, and prompting statements out loud.

(continues)

Table 4.2
Steps for Implementing a Cognitive
Behavior Modification Program *Continued.*

---

4. Self-Management Independence Training

The student practices the strategy under teacher direction, beginning
with overt speech and fading to covert speech. The session begins with
a review of on- and off-task behaviors, purpose (to stay on task), and
goal of the strategy (to complete assigned work during seatwork time
and self-monitor behavior). The steps to be followed during the process
(self-monitoring, self-recording, and self-rewarding) are also reviewed.
Finally, the student discusses the strategy aloud using the videotape,
timing signal, and self-monitoring sheet. The student continues this
process with overt speech until the process has become routine and the
student is using it accurately. When the student follows the process correctly, he or she is instructed to fade overt speech to whispering, then to
covert or silent speech. The teacher provides continual feedback on student progress.

At this point, the student no longer self-monitors on-task behavior on
videotape but uses the strategy during seatwork time. The timing device and self-monitoring sheet are placed on the student's desk. The
teacher may elect to continue to videotape seatwork for 3 to 5 days to
allow the student to see progress. In addition, the teacher collects daily
data on student behavior to establish strategy efficacy. The teacher may
choose to discontinue daily data collection when the strategy appears to
be working. However, the teacher continues to monitor that the student
is using the strategy correctly and maintaining on-task behavior.

5. Treatment Withdrawal

The ultimate goal of this strategy is to allow the student to independently engage in the targeted behavior at an acceptable rate. Thus, for
this strategy to be deemed effective, the teacher's role in the program
should be faded. Fading should be done with the same careful consideration that went into the initial stages of discrimination training, self-
management implementation, and self-management independence
training. That is, the student should be able to initiate and complete
the strategy without teacher assistance, even though the teacher continually monitors the targeted behavior. An increase in inappropriate
behavior requires reevaluation and readjustment of the withdrawal
process. Student readiness for generalization is also evaluated.

6. Generalization Training

Generalization training allows the student to self-monitor the targeted
behavior across different subject areas, activities, classrooms, or all three.
In addition, it may help the student to target other, similar behaviors for
which the strategy may be appropriate. Instruction at this stage assumes

---

(continues)

Table 4.2
Steps for Implementing a Cognitive
Behavior Modification Program *Continued.*

---

6. Generalization Training *Continued.*

the same degree of importance as in the training phase. Unless the student is taught to use and modify the strategy as needed, lasting behavior change has not occurred.

Note. Adapted from "Implementing Cognitive Behavior Management Programs for Persons with Autism: Guidelines for Practitioners," by C. Quinn, B. L. Swaggart, and B. S. Myles, 1994, *Focus on Autistic Behavior, 9*(4), pp. 5–12. Copyright 1994 by PRO-ED, Inc. Adapted with permission.

desired behavior by following the desired behavior with either a positive consequence or removal of an unpleasant stimulus. For obvious reasons, the latter option is less preferred. Based on a thorough environmental and functional analysis of behavior, three forms of positive reinforcement have particular utility with children and youth with Asperger Syndrome: contingent activities, social consequences, and token economy systems (see Table 4.3).

As previously suggested, reinforcement programs may be best implemented through collaborative social contracts in which adults and the students with Asperger Syndrome clearly define their goals, expectations, and consequences. Students should receive reinforcers that are extremely powerful and motivating. Reinforcers should be offered in menus from which the student may select. Menus should be rotated frequently to ensure that students do not become sated on a particular reinforcer. These programs are frequently most effective when the students are permitted to apply them through self-management and other cognitive-based methods.

Behavior Contracts

Behavior, or contingency, contracts offer the teacher and the student with Asperger Syndrome a flexible means of addressing individual needs. For example, a contract may be used to teach new behaviors, maintain existing behaviors, extinguish undesirable behaviors, or provide enrichment opportunities. A behavior contract is an agreement among parties (e.g., teacher, student, parents) that specific behaviors will result in specific

Table 4.3
Types of Reinforcers

Reinforcer	Description
Contingent activities	This reinforcer makes certain preferred events (e.g., computer time) contingent on an individual's satisfactorily meeting some previously specified level of performance or behavior. For instance, after meeting a prescribed standard of academic work and behavior, a child might be permitted to work on a puzzle in the free-time area of his classroom. Children and youth with Asperger Syndrome often have strong (albeit sometimes unusual) preferences for alone time and frequently benefit from the structure inherent in following adult-directed activities with preferred activities, which makes this a particularly effective tool.
Social consequences	Adults and peers offer contingent, supportive, and constructive verbal and nonverbal feedback. This tool is powerful if the student with Asperger Syndrome understands the social behavior being communicated and the reason it is being communicated. Social consequences must be overtly used with careful definitions so that the student can interpret them correctly. This can be one of the most effective ways of positively influencing the behavior and social development of individuals with Asperger Syndrome.
Token economy systems	This reinforcer involves the use of items such as chips, play money, and points that are redeemable for a variety of desired items. Token systems are extremely adaptable and offer several advantages for children and youth with Asperger Syndrome: (a) They can be used to support and complement other forms of reinforcement, including contingent activities and social consequences; (b) tokens can be backed up by a variety of reinforcers and are less subject to satiation than other types of reinforcement; (c) tokens can be given without disrupting desired target responses (e.g., a student can be given a chip for appropriate social behavior without interfering with a social activity); (d) tokens allow several individuals with different reinforcement preferences to flexibly use the same program; (e) tokens can be used by professionals, parents, and others; and (f) tokens earned can serve as an empirical basis for evaluating program progress.

consequences. The contract focuses on positive outcomes, and skills and consequences (typically in the form of reinforcement menus) are stated in a manner that leads the student to success. Downing (1990) outlined the steps needed to develop, implement, and monitor a behavior contract. These guidelines are listed in Table 4.4.

Antecedent Intervention Programs

Antecedent intervention programs may also be designed to successfully manage the behavior of children and youth with Asperger Syndrome. Antecedent modification does not rely on manipulation of consequences. Instead, it structures environmental conditions to reduce the probability of a behavior's occurring. For example, a child with Asperger Syndrome who demonstrates her

Table 4.4
Steps for Developing, Implementing,
and Monitoring a Behavior Contract

1. **Meet with Concerned Parties**

   The student, teacher(s), and parent(s) who will be supporting the contract meet to discuss one target behavior.

2. **Determine Conditions**

   The parties determine when, where, and under what specific conditions the behavior occurs. The contract will be written to address these conditions.

3. **Determine Who Will Use the Contract and Where It Will Be Used**

   All persons who will be responsible for contract implementation must know their responsibilities.

4. **Determine Reinforcement**

   Students should be allowed to participate in developing a menu of reinforcers. Reinforcers should be manageable but powerful enough to evoke the desired response. Menus should be rotated often to ensure that student motivation remains high.

5. **Determine Whether Negative Consequences Will Be Used**

   Contracts are written in a positive way to increase behaviors. Negative reinforcers may not be necessary or even desirable if the positive reinforcers are motivating for the student.

(continues)

Table 4.4
Steps for Developing, Implementing, and Monitoring a Behavior Contract *Continued.*

---

6. Take Baseline Data

The parties determine the frequency with which the behavior occurs. Data should be taken over at least 3 to 5 days to ensure that the behavior is typical for the student.

7. Determine Reinforcement Schedule

The parties determine how often the student is to receive reinforcers. The contract should be structured so that the student has a successful experience; this will prompt the student to further work toward the contract goals.

8. Determine Goals

The parties determine the criteria for successful completion of the contract. Realistic and reasonable goals should be set, even if those goals do not represent the final level of expectation for the student. When the student consistently reaches the goals, the contract can be modified to target a higher goal.

9. Write the Contract

The contract should be written in terms that specify task and time demands, criteria for accuracy, and available reinforcers.

10. Discuss and Sign the Contract

All concerned parties discuss the contract to ensure understanding. It might be necessary to supplement a discussion with drawings or icons for some students with Asperger Syndrome. All concerned parties should receive a copy of the contract.

11. Monitor the Contract

The parties set up a plan to evaluate and modify the contract if needed. All concerned parties should remain in regular contact with one another to ensure that student progress across settings is monitored. If the contract is unsuccessful, the parties need to address task appropriateness, time allotment, and student or environmental factors that could have impeded student progress.

Note. Adapted from "Contingency Contracts: A Step-by-Step Format," by J. A. Downing, 1990, *Intervention in School and Clinic, 26*(2), 111–113. Copyright 1990 by PRO-ED, Inc. Adapted with permission.

concern over hallway noises by tuning out might best be dealt with by moving her desk away from the source of the noise, as opposed to designing consequences to modify the unwanted behavior. A student who regularly displayes verbally inappropriate behavior and occasional aggression related to frustration associated with not understanding abstract algebra equations and geometry concepts might be successfully assigned to another math class. Thus, rather than applying consequences for unacceptable behavior, antecedent manipulation measures involve modifying or mitigating those variables that are associated with the problem. Myriad variables can be used to create favorable antecedent conditions, including curricula and structuring methods.

Behavior Reduction Strategies

Behavior reduction strategies involve presenting undesired consequences or withdrawing reinforcement when individuals display specified undesired behaviors. Behavior reduction methods are appropriate only when it can be confirmed that students are able to perform a desired behavior. That is, it is inappropriate to present undesired consequences or withdraw reinforcement in instances where students are unable to perform the desired response. Parents and educators should carefully consider when or whether they should use behavior reduction approaches with children and youth with Asperger Syndrome. Although these strategies can be effective for some of these children, they are often perceived by students as a form of top–down management and result in additional negative behavior and power struggles. Behavior reduction strategies that may be appropriate for children and youth with Asperger Syndrome include differential reinforcement, response cost, and time-out (see Table 4.5).

If behavior reduction strategies are used, positive alternatives should generally be implemented first. In addition, these guidelines should be followed:

- Implement behavior reduction programs through collaborative social contracts that clearly spell out goals, expectations, and consequences.

- Apply consequences in a firm, predictable, and direct manner.

- Whenever possible, attempt to implement behavior reduction programs through self-management and other cognitive-based methods. For example, a child might be trained to quietly lay her head on her desk for 2 minutes when she displays a particular unacceptable behavior.

Table 4.5
Behavior Reduction Methods

Method	Description
Differential reinforcement of other behavior (DRO)	This method attends to and rewards behaviors that are not displayed for specified periods of time. That is, reinforcement is contingent upon the nonoccurrence of a particular response.
Differential reinforcement of alternative behavior (DRA)	This method attends to and rewards behaviors that are more appropriate alternatives or forms of a behavior. This form of differential reinforcement may involve shaping and redirecting a student with Asperger Syndrome.
Differential reinforcement of incompatible behavior (DRI)	This method attends to and rewards behaviors that are incompatible with the undesired behavior. Reinforcing a student who experiences difficulty in keeping his hands off other students when he is standing in line for keeping his hands in his pocket is a common DRI program, because having hands in pockets is incompatible with touching others.
Differential reinforcement of lower rates of behavior (DRL)	This form of differential reinforcement offers reinforcement for behaviors that occur less than or equal to a specified limit. Thus, DRL programs systematically lower acceptable rates of a target behavior. These programs are particularly effective with students who are interested in behavioral self-monitoring.
Response cost	This method reduces undesired behaviors by removing a reinforcer whenever the undesired behavior is observed. Thus, preferred activities, privileges, free time, and even tokens may be withdrawn when the undesired behavior is displayed. When used in conjunction with reinforcement programs, and when target behaviors are carefully selected to shape desired responses, response cost programs can be effective. For instance, such a program was used in conjunction with a token system and peer-mediated social interaction program to assist a student in remembering not to stroke the faces of peers in her classroom. That is, she was reinforced for standing an appropriate distance from her peers and not touching their faces when talking with them;

(continues)

Table 4.5
Behavior Reduction Methods *Continued.*

Method	Description
	when she did touch their faces, she had a chip removed from her "reinforcement box."
Time-out	This method involves removing an individual from a preferred situation when specified unacceptable behaviors are displayed. Time-out is most effective when (a) it is used with limited numbers of specified unacceptable behaviors (as opposed to being used with a variety of behaviors); (b) when it is for brief periods (typically, 2 minutes is adequate time away from ongoing classroom activities); and (c) it is carefully and empirically evaluated for efficacy. For example, a youth with Asperger Syndrome was required to place materials he was using on the floor under his desk and to place his head on his desk without talking or making noises for 2 minutes when he spit in the classroom.

- As much as possible, avoid communication and interactions that create opportunities for power struggles and confrontations.
- Be sensitive to conflicts related to behavior reduction strategies that may escalate into a crisis.

Behavior reduction strategies should generally be used only under the following conditions: (a) when positive reinforcement methods have not been successful, or when the nature or severity of a behavior necessitates a more immediate response; (b) if incompatible desired behaviors occur too infrequently (or cannot be sufficiently shaped) to serve as the focus of reinforcement; (c) if an undesired behavior is so intense as to be a danger to an individual; and (d) only when paired with positive reinforcement for desired behavior and systematically, promptly, and consistently carried out in accordance with an approved, written positive behavior support plan by well-trained professionals, staff, or parents or a combination thereof. The plan should include a clear, specific description of what is to be done, who will execute the plan, how long the procedures will be in force, and how the program's success will be evaluated.

Power Struggles and Aggression Among Students with Asperger Syndrome

It is common for adults who manage and interact with children and youth with Asperger Syndrome to become entrapped in power struggles, frivolous arguments, and other nonproductive confrontations. Unfortunately, at least some of these situations may escalate into crises. For example, one teacher described her frustration in attempting to convince a youth with Asperger Syndrome of the necessity of regular bathing and personal hygiene. In an attempt to convince him of the advantages of good personal hygiene, she said that the youth would be unable to get a good job if he failed to follow accepted hygiene practices. The youth's response was that he intended to pursue a career as a home-based computer programmer. He argued that because he would not be around other people, there was no reason for him to bathe. The teacher then argued that his ability to find a date for the spring dance would be enhanced if he regularly showered and used deodorant. The youth's response to this argument was that he had no interest in attending the school dance but intended to stay home and work on his computer. The teacher reported that this scenario was typical of her interactions with the student. He was highly skilled at entrapping the teacher in power struggles and unproductive arguments that occasionally escalated into major confrontations and crises. Following are some suggestions for avoiding these common problems.

- Describe in direct terms the behaviors you want the student to display, behaviors about which you are concerned, or both. Inherent in this recommendation is the idea that the child will focus on the behavior of concern rather than on the social consequences of the behavior.
- Avoid suggestive and indirect language. Such language not only is difficult for many individuals with Asperger Syndrome to understand but also creates opportunities for power struggles and confrontations. For example, when a student says to a teacher, "I think you

are stupid," the teacher should not attribute meaning to the statement by saying, "Why are you upset with me?" The student might not have been upset with the teacher in the first place, but given this lead may pursue it and thereby mask the real intention behind the statement.

• Be sensitive to the fact that many individuals with Asperger Syndrome may appear to lack emotion. Many of these children and youth are unable to understand and show their emotions. Thus, when under stress or when confronted with conflict, they may appear to be emotionally detached or calm. In these situations, teachers and parents may fail to recognize that the child is experiencing significant stress and emotion that he or she is unable to communicate and overtly manifest. As a result, an interaction may escalate into a bigger problem or even a crisis.

• Apply consistent, firm, and controlled interventions. Adults who interact with children and youth with Asperger Syndrome need to be able to apply firm and predictable directives and consequences. Harsh, punitive, and unexpected directives and consequences often provoke power struggles and increased problems. Moreover, negative and confrontational responses may result in crises.

Children and youth diagnosed with Asperger Syndrome are not inherently aggressive. Nevertheless, problems of aggression among these students are relatively common. The social deficits and excesses connected with Asperger Syndrome, such as difficulties in engaging in age-appropriate reciprocal play and other social interactions, frequently create problems and frustrations that mushroom into aggressive and violent responses and counteractions. For instance, a child with Asperger Syndrome may experience difficulties interacting with peers as a result of not understanding commonly known and accepted social rules, thereby giving the appearance of being rude or unwilling to follow the rules of generally understood games. Problems may also arise when these children and youth are unable to recognize and respond to peers' subtle social cues, for example, when a nondisabled peer tries to communicate to a child with Asperger Syndrome that she is standing too close during a game or conversation.

Related difficulties, such as attending and responding to salient social cues, connecting these cues to previous social experiences; self-monitoring behavioral and social responses; rigidly attempting to apply social rules that are highly variable; and displaying poor empathy, social and emotional stiffness, and social awkwardness, may further exacerbate the behavioral and social problems of students with Asperger Syndrome and thereby increase the likelihood that they will become involved in confrontational and aggressive situations. Furthermore, the emotional and social vulnerability and stress that are common among individuals with Asperger Syndrome make them prone to aggressive outbursts as well as targets for bullying and exploitation.

Because of their unique social and behavioral characteristics, students with Asperger Syndrome are apt to be responsive to therapeutic strategies that may be different from those used with students with other types of disabilities. Strategies exclusively or primarily based on punitive measures typically do not work well for students with Asperger Syndrome. Such strategies almost always fail to address the underlying causes of these individuals' problems, including stress, poor problem-solving ability, poor organizational skills, and problems in predicting outcomes of social responses. Accordingly, students with Asperger Syndrome often manifest aggression because they have difficulty understanding and functioning in a world they perceive to be threatening, inconsistent, and unpredictable.

As suggested throughout this book, students with Asperger Syndrome require management programming that is uniquely crafted to meet their individual needs. Such programming should include (a) the support of structured environments, (b) opportunities to participate in cognitively based management programs, and (c) the support of faculty and staff who are knowledgeable and skilled in dealing with power struggles and violence.

• *Structured environments.* An essential element of an individualized management program that may curtail aggression is a structured environment. As suggested numerous times, children and youth with Asperger Syndrome can be expected to have fewer episodes involving aggression and other behavioral problems and more positive social interactions and school experiences when they are provided clear and consistent guidelines and support for appropriate behavior. Such guidelines and support are most effective when accompanied by clear models of acceptable behavior, opportunities to practice desired behavior, and feedback for acceptable and unacceptable performance. These students also tend to respond to programs that incorporate ongoing rule monitoring and maintenance of consistent behavioral expectations. Thus, routines and schedules can provide order, consistency, and structure for these students. Moreover, physical, environmental, cognitive, and attitudinal supports are essential in assisting these students in preventing and managing episodes of aggression. In this regard, students with Asperger Syndrome function best in settings where adults and peers understand their disability and where adequate resources exist to effectively manage and supervise them.

For example, a somewhat peculiarly acting student with Asperger Syndrome is often teased for the way she dresses and talks and is generally made fun of in the hallways of her school. In response to these situations, she sometimes screams and attempts to hit her harassers. These incidents often result in her being punished. In response to these problems, she and her teacher make a card for her to carry to remind her of appropriate choices of behaviors in response to teasing. This simple environmental support—applied in conjunction with other supports, including the education of her peers regarding Asperger Syndrome and consequences for harassment—proves to be an effective intervention.

• *Cognitive-based management programs.* Opportunities to participate in cognitive-based management programs are also important in managing the aggressive responses sometimes seen in students with Asperger Syndrome. These methods generally empower the students to self-evaluate and self-manage, so they can avoid the often poor outcomes associated with relying on top–down management programs for students with Asperger Syndrome. Some students with Asperger Syndrome may respond positively to top–down strategies; however, there is strong evidence that many will resist or be unresponsive to them. Hence, as noted previously, it is generally recommended that management programs for these students be crafted to counter aggression by being cognitively based. Cognitive behavior modification programs, behavioral contracts, social stories, social scripts, cartoon analyses, social autopsies, and similar methods are particularly appropriate.

• *Knowledgeable and skilled faculty and staff.* Students with Asperger Syndrome do best when supported by faculty and staff who are knowledgeable and skilled in dealing with power struggles and violence. Students with Asperger Syndrome are well known for being adept at creating power struggles with adults. Moreover, when trapped in power struggles and confrontations, students with Asperger Syndrome are more prone to acts of aggression. Accordingly, it is essential that school personnel design and implement programs so that they reduce opportunities for power struggles. The following are particularly recommended: (a) Describe in specific terms the behaviors you want the student to display or about which you are concerned, rather than the social consequences of the behavior; (b) avoid emotion-loaded questions (e.g., "Why are you upset with me?") and instead ask the student to describe the event so that you can search for antecedents or triggers; (c) recognize that children and youth with Asperger Syndrome may appear to be unable to understand and show their emotions. When under stress or when confronted with conflict, these students may appear to be emotionally detached or calm. In such situations, adults may not recognize that these individuals are actually experiencing such significant stress and emotion that they may be unable to communicate.

To be effective in managing students prone to aggressive responses, educators and others must also consistently apply firm and predictable consequences and avoid using punitive, harsh, and unanticipated consequences that often provoke power struggles and increase the likelihood of aggression.

Concluding Thoughts

Children and youth with Asperger Syndrome are well known for their behavioral excesses and deficits. An essential aspect of planning and programming for these students involves development, implementation, and evaluation of effective management tools. Management tools for children and youth with Asperger Syndrome clearly define and explain class rules, teacher expectations, and environmental constraints and structure. Also, supports help individuals with Asperger Syndrome begin to recognize that they can request modifications or restructure their environment as needed. Therefore, self-monitoring and cognitive-based methods based on collaboratively developed social contracts used in combination with structured environments and related supports are highly recommended.

Planning for Social Success   5

Professionals and parents alike consider social interaction opportunities and social skills development to be essential for children and youth with Asperger Syndrome. In fact, many believe that this is the most distinctive characteristic of individuals with Asperger Syndrome (Church, Alisanski, & Amanullah, 2000; Joliffe & Baron-Cohen, 1999; McLaughlin-Cheng, 1998; Myles & Southwick, 1999). Researchers and practitioners have discussed the negative impact of not having appropriate social skills, ranging from not being able to develop and keep friendships to being ridiculed by peers to not being able to keep a job because of lack of understanding of workplace culture and relationships among subordinates and supervisors (Baron-Cohen, O'Riordan, Stone, Jones, & Plaisted, 1999; Joliffe & Baron-Cohen, 1999; MacLeod, 1999; Mawhood & Howlin, 1999).

Social skills comprise a complex area of human behavior. Although somewhat rule governed, the rules vary across location, situations, people, age, and culture, making it difficult to acquire and subsequently generalize these skills. Greeting is one example of a social skill that is thought to be simple. However, further analysis shows that this skill, which most take for granted, is extremely complex. How a child greets a friend in the classroom differs from how he or she greets the friend at the local mall. The

---

Note. Portions of this chapter are from "Understanding the Hidden Curriculum: An Essential Social Skill for Children and Youth with Asperger Syndrome," by B. S. Myles and R. L. Simpson, 2001, *Intervention in School and Clinic, 36*(5), pp. 279–286. Copyright 2001 by PRO-ED, Inc. Reprinted with permission.

greeting used the first time the child sees a friend differs from the greeting exchange when they see each other 30 minutes later. Also, the words and actions used in greetings differ depending on whether the child is greeting a teacher or a peer. Greetings are thus complex, as are most social skills.

General Principles of Social Skills Development

As previously observed, social interaction problems are often extreme for individuals with Asperger Syndrome. Accordingly, increasing the quantity and quality of social interactions for children with Asperger Syndrome is of paramount concern. Several general principles can serve as foundation elements for a program to develop social skills.

▶ Principle 1

Although social interaction problems of individuals with Asperger Syndrome are often described as mild social norm deviations, this perception should in no way diminish the significance of these problems. Individuals with Asperger Syndrome are not known for extremely deviant behavior, such as self-injury, highly aberrant self-stimulatory behaviors, or bizarre responses. Rather, they tend to be socially different or slightly quirky in their behavior. The problems evidenced in this characteristic pattern are often perceived to be relatively unimportant or easily corrected. It is not unusual for parents and professionals to expect that students with Asperger Syndrome will be able to easily self-correct their own behavior and to believe that the social consequences of these so-called mild difficulties are relatively unimportant. There is overwhelming evidence that there are severe social consequences applied to individuals with Asperger Syndrome. Although it is true that the behavior of individuals with Asperger Syndrome appear to be less atypical than the extreme responses of some children with autism spectrum disorders, this in no way should be perceived to attenuate the impact of these difficulties.

▶ Principle 2

Social interaction skills must be explicitly taught to students with Asperger Syndrome, and the students' peers must also be taught social interaction support behaviors. Communicating to a student with Asperger Syndrome that his behavior is unacceptable without explicitly providing a more appropriate alternative behavior, or otherwise failing to instruct the individual in making a desired response, is clearly ineffective. Children and youth with Asperger Syndrome can acquire desired social skills only when adults and peers with whom they interact offer appropriate direct instruction, including strategies for skill generalization and maintenance. Furthermore, peers and adults who have opportunities to interact with persons with Asperger Syndrome must be instructed in how to support and maintain these desired responses, including serving as age-appropriate behavior models, providing feedback related to acceptable and unacceptable behavior, and using contingent social reinforcement. Finally, it is painfully apparent that, without education and training, many peers of students with Asperger Syndrome can be expected to ignore, bully, and discriminate against their special-needs classmates. That students with Asperger Syndrome are able to demonstrate significant progress when suitable instruction, models, and related supports are provided by peers makes it clear that an effective social interaction program must include a significant measure of peer training and support.

▶ Principle 3

Parents, professionals, and peers must be assisted in developing and maintaining reasonable social skills expectations for individuals with Asperger Syndrome. Asperger Syndrome is a severe, lifelong social disability. Accordingly, even under optimal conditions, it is unreasonable to expect that these children will completely overcome their disability or that social skills will somehow become a relative strength. Acceptance of this circumstance should in no way diminish high expectations for these students or detract from expected outcomes. It does, however, remind educators and parents involved in the lives of children and youth with Asperger Syndrome that education and training are tools that are used to support individuals with this exceptionality, rather than strategies that can be used to "cure" them of their social difficulties. Just as it would be unrealistic to expect that a child with a severe form of spina bifida could become an Olympic sprinter, it would be equally unrealistic to expect that a child with Asperger Syndrome could achieve goals that require outstanding social skills. Nonetheless, such children can be taught social skills that will allow them to achieve fulfilling social outcomes.

▶ Principle 4

High-quality reciprocal social interactions are most apt to occur in the absence of aggression and grossly unacceptable behaviors. Peers of students with Asperger Syndrome are fundamental to these students' engaging in quality social interactions and developing needed social skills. Indeed, without participation of peers there are severe limitations on the development of social skills by students with Asperger Syndrome. Many peers of individuals with Asperger Syndrome are interested and willing to participate in social support programs. Even in the most positive of environments, however, these peers will generally be intolerant of aggression and overtly atypical behaviors. For example, students who chronically spit, hit, or kick others; display sexual behaviors in public; and so forth will create significant barriers to social interaction. Accordingly, adults who coordinate social interaction support and training programs must be in a position to limit these interfering behaviors. Ideally, these behaviors should be eliminated or significantly reduced prior to program initiation.

▶ Principle 5

Skill-training targets must be carefully selected to maximize their potential social impact. There is no question that individuals who are involved in educating or parenting children with Asperger Syndrome have myriad social targets from which to choose, because individuals with Asperger Syndrome often experience numerous excesses and deficits within various social domains. However, helping a child with Asperger Syndrome to appropriately use a social skill in a variety of settings is no easy matter. There are typically significant time and effort costs associated with this support. Therefore, it is imperative that social skills targets have clear and practical social validity. Any social skill taught to a student with Asperger Syndrome should have the potential to yield clear social benefit. Skills that are particularly noteworthy are those that are fundamental and pivotal to a number of domains. Thus, skills that are easily taught and those that may be conveniently used to demonstrate program efficacy or success are not always the most suitable for training.

The Hidden Curriculum

One important social skills area that has long been neglected is "the hidden curriculum," the do's and don'ts for everyday behavior that are not spelled out but everyone somehow knows about (Bieber, 1994)—except for children and youth with Asperger Syndrome. The hidden curriculum includes skills, actions, modes of dress, and so on, that most people know and take for granted. Every society and every school has a hidden curriculum. This unspoken curriculum is the one that causes challenges—and, indeed, grief—for those with Asperger Syndrome.

> In the halls at school, the hidden curriculum is in operation. Before school, Mark saunters up to Sam, a third-grade student with Asperger Syndrome, and says, "How's it hangin' dog?" Sam gets extremely upset and yells, "I am not a dog!" Mark, who was merely using the latest "in" greeting, shrugs his shoulders and comments to a friend walking with him, "Man, he's weird. Just gonna stay out of his way." Sam, on the other hand, remains unsettled until he has an opportunity to meet with his resource teacher, Mrs. Miller, at 10:30. During a 15-minute discussion, his teacher interprets the situation for him and helps him to understand that Mark was just saying a friendly hello. When Sam asks Mrs. Miller how she and the other kids have learned that greeting, Mrs. Miller shrugs her shoulders, unable to come up with a response.

In yet another example, everyone knows that Mrs. Robbins allows students to whisper in class as long as they get their work done, whereas Mrs. Cook does not tolerate any level of noise in her class. Similarly, everyone knows that Mr. Johnson, the assistant principal, is a stickler for following the rules, so no one curses or even slouches in his presence. Everyone also knows that the really tough guys (the ones who like to beat up unsuspecting kids) hang out behind the slide, just out of teacher view—everyone knows these things—everyone, that is, except the student with Asperger Syndrome.

Outside of school, the hidden curriculum is an even bigger issue. What is the hidden curriculum for talking to or taking rides from strangers? The bus driver is a stranger, but it is permissible to accept a ride from her. It is not okay to ride with the stranger who pulls up to the curb and stops. The cashier at the grocery store is a stranger, but it is acceptable to make small talk with him. It is not okay, however, to divulge personal information to someone who is standing in the produce section. It is okay to accept candy from the distributor who is giving free samples at Toys"R"Us, yet it is not prudent to take candy from a stranger standing on the street corner.

Individuals with Asperger Syndrome need to know never to argue with a policeman. They also need to know (a) teacher expectations, (b) teacher-pleasing behaviors, (c) which students to interact with and which to stay away from, and (d) behaviors that attract both positive and negative attention. Understanding the hidden curriculum can make all the difference to students with Asperger Syndrome—it can keep them out of detention, or worse, and it can help them make friends.

The hidden curriculum covers a multitude of areas. For some of these, a generous investment of time is required to ensure that the student understands; other "rules" can be learned in a matter of minutes. As previously stated, the hidden curriculum varies across location, situations, people, age, and culture. Therefore, it is impossible to generate a comprehensive list that applies to all students with Asperger Syndrome in all situations. Table 5.1 provides some examples of hidden curriculum items that can serve as a starting point for helping individuals with this exceptionality understand this very complex topic.

Table 5.1
Examples of Hidden Curriculum Items

- Do not tell the principal that if she listened better more kids would like her.
- You should not have to pay students to be your friends.
- Do not talk to other kids in the classroom when the teacher is giving a lesson.
- When the teacher is scolding another student, it is not an appropriate time to ask the teacher a question.
- When you are with classmates you don't know very well and you are the center of attention, do not pass gas, pick your nose, or scratch a private body part.
- During a fire drill, go with your class to the nearest exit. This is not the time to go to the bathroom or to ask to go to the bathroom.
- Do not tell classmates about the "skeletons in your parents' closets."
- Do not draw violent scenes in school.
- During a conversation, face the speaker and position your body in that direction.
- Speak to teachers in a pleasant tone of voice, because they will respond to you in a more positive manner.
- When your teacher gives you a warning about behavior and you continue the behavior, you are probably going to get into trouble. If you stop the behavior immediately after the first warning, you will probably not get into trouble.
- If one of your classmates tells you to do something you think might get you into trouble, you should always stop and think before acting. Friends do not ask other friends to do things that will get them into trouble.
- Not all teachers have the same rules for their class. Some teachers do not allow any talking unless you raise your hand. Others may allow talking if you are not disruptive and annoying other students. It is important to know the rules different teachers have for their class.

Note. Adapted from "Understanding the Hidden Curriculum: An Essential Social Skill for Children and Youth with Asperger Syndrome," by B. S. Myles and R. L. Simpson, 2001, *Intervention in School and Clinic, 36*(5), p. 282. Copyright 2001 by PRO-ED, Inc. Adapted with permission.

Social Interventions

Developing appropriate social skills and facilitating positive and productive social interactions between children and youth diagnosed with Asperger Syndrome and others is no easy task. However, certain methods have proved effective. Social skills training, including teaching the hidden curriculum, needs to be approached systematically by individuals who teach children and youth with Asperger Syndrome. It is best addressed through a process of instruction and interpretation.

Instruction

Instruction includes providing direct assistance in acquiring skills. Instructional components may include (a) scope and sequence, (b) direct instruction, (c) social stories, (d) social scripts, (e) acting lessons, (f) self-esteem building, (g) the Power Card, (h) strategies for positive social peer contacts, (i) adult-mediated strategies, and (j) peer-mediated strategies.

Scope and Sequence

Because children and youth with Asperger Syndrome evidence an uneven profile of social skills, it is important to understand the sequence in which these skills develop. Without an understanding of scope and sequence, one may fail to realize that a child is missing an important prerequisite skill that might make the child learn a more advanced skill by rote, thereby precluding it from becoming a usable asset. For example, if a student does not understand that tone of voice communicates a message, then teaching the more advanced skill of using a respectful tone of voice to teachers may have little or no meaning. That is, if the student learns by rote to use that tone of voice, it most likely will not be generalized to other settings.

There are several scopes and sequences that outline skills that specifically support self-awareness, self-calming, and self-management. For example, Howlin, Baron-Cohen, and Hadwin (1999) and Goldstein and McGinnis (1997) provided a sequence of development and instructional strategies to promote social and emotional understanding.

Direct Instruction

Relative to increasing the quantity and quality of peer interactions and developing social skills, direct instruction refers to directly guiding children in desired responses. Thus, the first step in direct instruction is to identify the desired social interaction or social skill goal (e.g., playing a cooperative, age-appropriate board game with a peer). Second, the steps the child takes to reach the goal are identified (e.g., approach a peer with an invitation to play, obtain the game from its designated storage space, ask the peer to choose a color for game pieces, and so forth). Third, these steps are sequentially taught to the child using best-practices methods. Such methods include modeling (e.g., demonstrating the desired social behavior related to the board game); providing multiple opportunities to practice desired behaviors (e.g., allowing the child to practice playing the board game with teachers and others before playing the game with peers); providing instructional prompts (e.g., prompting the child to drop dice on the board and move her game piece the correct number of spaces); reinforcing desired behaviors (e.g., praising the child for cooperatively playing the game with a peer); and providing multiple opportunities to engage in the desired behavior (e.g., giving the child opportunities to play board games with different peers at different times of the day). Following is an example of direct instruction on participating in a group leisure activity.

▶ Direct Instruction of a Leisure Skill

In an effort to develop a social activity in which Alex could participate during recess, Mr. Goldberg selected "four-square," an activity Alex and his classmates enjoyed and commonly participated in. Mr. Goldberg analyzed the skills needed by Alex to participate in this activity: (a) identify one or more partners, (b) request that they join in playing four-square, (c) follow rules of the game (e.g., play fair, take turns), and (d) put away materials when directed by a teacher or at the conclusion of recess. Mr. Goldberg then taught the skills to Alex, first by modeling them and then by asking Alex to role-play the steps with him. Next, he gave Alex opportunities to practice the new skills with

different peers and teachers. During this time, Mr. Goldberg
provided prompts and reinforcement to Alex as needed, thus
ensuring that he had multiple opportunities to use these
new skills during various recess periods.

A primary advantage of direct instruction is that it is based
on methods that have been empirically shown to have social validity. The primary disadvantage is that direct instruction of social interaction skills does not always generalize to other settings and situations. That is, a child who is taught to play a
particular board game with a limited number of students in her
classroom may show little interest in playing similar games or
engaging in alternative peer activities, playing with new children, or engaging in the desired behavior outside her classroom.
Thus, social skills training based on direct instruction must be
geared to respond to these potential problems.

Most social skills curricula cover subject matter that can be
delivered using a direct instruction model. For example, Duke,
Nowicki, and Martin (1996) provided a school-based curriculum to
teach nonverbal language in the areas of (a) paralanguage, (b) facial expression, (c) space and touch, (d) gestures and postures,
(e) rhythm and time, and (f) personal hygiene. Shure (1992) approached social skills from a problem-solving view, providing direct instruction on (a) pre–problem-solving skills, (b) alternative
solutions, (c) consequences, (d) solution–consequence pairs, and
(d) means–end thinking.

Social Stories

Because of their relatively strong cognitive and language skills,
children and adolescents with Asperger Syndrome often benefit
from the structure imposed by self-instructional and self-control
problem-solving procedures. That is, they are often able to profit
from strategies based on directives and guidance for responding
to various situations. One of the most promising of these options
is social stories (Gray & Garand, 1993; Hagiwara & Myles, 1999;
Norris & Dattilo, 1999; Rogers & Myles, 2001; Swaggart et al.,
1995). A social story describes social situations specific to individuals and circumstances. For instance, a social story might be
developed for a youth who attends a general education English
class. The story includes a description of the youth, the setting,
peers and adults associated with the setting, and the youth's

feelings and perceptions related to the setting (e.g., the youth likes to read and write in his class journal). There are also directive statements that describe appropriate behaviors for the setting (e.g., upon entering the classroom, the youth should sit at his desk and take out his textbook, and until the bell rings he may quietly talk to people seated near him). Thus, this method involves structuring an individual's behavior and social responses by offering individualized, specific response cues. Although the empirical efficacy of social stories has not been definitively established, preliminary indications are that it may be a beneficial method of offering structure for many children and youth with Asperger Syndrome. Following are two examples of social stories. The first was developed for a child to assist him with problems he experienced during lunch; the second, for a youth who was of concern to parents and classmates because of her poor personal hygiene.

▶ Lunch Behavior

Every day I look forward to lunch. Lunch is a time I get to eat and to be with other children in Ms. Zenith's class. At 12 noon Ms. Zenith announces that it is time to get ready for lunch. When she tells me, I get my lunch from my locker and walk to the cafeteria. Sometimes the cafeteria is noisy. I can sit at any table during lunch time. I like to sit with my friends. When I am finished with my lunch, I throw away my trash. When the bell rings, I go back to my locker and get ready for my next class.

▶ The Science of Sweat: Why I Need To Take a Shower and Use Deodorant Every Day

As a young adult, I am aware of how my body is changing and how this change is affecting me and other people. This awareness is important to me—I regularly think about it. Thinking and planning help me in my relationships with others.

One way my body has changed is in the area of sweating. All kids my age sweat, including the boys and girls who go to my school.

When boys and girls reach puberty, they begin to sweat more than when they were younger. Sometimes they sweat a lot. Sometimes they sweat a little. Most people sweat even when they don't feel hot.

Another name for sweat is perspiration. When perspiration comes out of our pores, it is clean. This sweat doesn't smell. Within seconds, however, bacteria appear and begin to live and grow in our perspiration.

These bacteria smell bad. It is best to wash these bacteria off every day. If we don't wash the bacteria off every day, more bacteria will come each day. Most people don't like the smell of other people's perspiration with bacteria in it. Most people think it smells really awful.

It is important to bathe and wash our armpits and genitals every day. If we cannot take a shower or bath, we can wash our armpits and genitals with a wet washcloth and soap. We can put deodorant in our armpits. If we are clean and wear deodorant, other people usually cannot smell the bacteria on our skin.

If we put deodorant in our armpits without washing off the bacteria, we will glue the bacteria from days before to ourselves. This will smell *really* bad.

It is also important to wear clean clothes. The sweat from our bodies gets into our clothes, especially the armpits of our shirts and the crotch of our underwear. Sometimes clothes we have worn for several hours or more may look clean, but they usually smell like bacteria, which is in the sweat. Most people don't like the smell of bacteria in sweat. In fact, most people think it smells really yucky!

After we shower or bathe, it is usually a good idea to put on clean clothes, especially a clean shirt and clean underwear. That way we will not get that bacteria back onto our bodies. That way others will not be able to smell yesterday's perspiration on our clothes.

Most people want to smell clean and fresh. We usually want others to think we smell clean and fresh, too. If we bathe or shower or wash carefully and wear clean underwear every day, we will feel more confident because we will smell clean and fresh.

Table 5.2 provides guidelines for social story construction for children and youth with Asperger Syndrome.

Table 5.2
Guidelines for Social Story Construction

1. **Identify a target behavior or problem situation for social story intervention.**

   The social story author should select a social behavior to be changed, preferably one whose improvement can result in increased positive social interactions, a safer environment, additional social learning opportunities, or all three. The behavior should be broken down into its component parts and based on the student's ability level. For example, during lunch Bob grabs food from his peers' plates and eats it. He exhibits this behavior at school, home, and restaurants. People who do not know Bob often react in a hostile manner. Accordingly, grabbing food from other people's plates is targeted for modification because it is socially unacceptable and interferes with development of more acceptable social contacts.

2. **Define target behavior for data collection.**

   For several reasons, it is imperative to clearly define the behavior on which data will be collected. Data collection is important for several reasons. First, all data collectors need an identical understanding of the targeted behavior to ensure reliability in measuring change. In addition, the behavior should be defined in such a way that the student understands the behavior to be exhibited. For example, Bob's current eating behavior consists of eating and grabbing. Eating is defined as sitting and consuming food only from the plate that is in front of him. Grabbing is defined as removing food from a plate other than his own.

3. **Collect baseline data on the target behavior.**

   Collecting data over an extended period allows the educator to determine a trend. Baseline data collection can last from 3 to 5 days or longer. To measure Bob's food-grabbing behavior, the observer can place a tally mark on a sheet of paper each time Bob grabs food from a peer's plate during lunch. The observer then logs the total number of tally marks onto a separate sheet of paper with the corresponding date.

4. **Write a short social story using descriptive, directive, and perspective sentences.**

   A good rule of thumb for writing social stories is to use descriptive and perspective sentences for every directive sentence in the story (Gray, 1994). Stories should be written in accordance with the student's comprehension skills, with vocabulary and print size individualized for each student. The stories should be written in the first person and in present or future tense (to describe a situation as it occurs or to anticipate an upcoming event, respectively). Students themselves may be involved in these activities.

(continues)

Table 5.2
Guidelines for Social Story Construction *Continued*.

5. **Choose the number of sentences per page according to the student's functioning level.**

Presentation of the social story is dependent on the student's functioning level. For some students, one to three sentences per page is adequate. Each sentence allows the student to focus on and process a specific concept. Depending on the student's skill level, more than one sentence per page may result in an overload of information such that the student does not comprehend the information.

6. **Use photographs, hand-drawn pictures, or pictorial icons.**

Pictures may enhance student understanding of appropriate behavior, especially with students who lack reading skills. For example, icons have been shown to be effective learning tools for children and youth. Gray (1994), however, cautioned that illustrations may too narrowly define a situation, resulting in limited generalization. Thus, decisions about whether to use pictures with social stories should be made on an individual basis. A picture on Bob's social story might depict him eating appropriately.

7. **Read the social story to the student and model the desired behavior.**

Reading the social story and modeling related behaviors as needed should become a consistent part of the student's daily schedule. For example, the story may be read just prior to the activity targeted by the story. Accordingly, Bob's story might be read to him right before lunch or at the beginning of the day to help him anticipate the situation and appropriate behavior. Depending on the student's functioning level, the teacher or the student may read the story. The student who is able to read independently may read the social story to peers so that all have a similar perspective of the targeted situation and appropriate behaviors.

8. **Collect intervention data.**

The educator should collect data throughout the social story program, using the procedures described for collecting and analyzing baseline data.

9. **Review the findings and related social story procedures.**

If the student does not respond with the desired behavior after approximately 2 weeks of the social story program, the person coordinating the intervention program should review the social story and its implementation procedures. It is recommended that if program alterations are made, only one variable should be changed at a time (e.g., change only

(continues)

Table 5.2
Guidelines for Social Story Construction *Continued.*

9. **Review the findings and related social story procedures.** *Continued.*

the content of the story, rather than simultaneously changing the time the story is read and the person who reads it). By changing only one factor at a time, the educator can determine the factor or factors that best facilitate a student's learning. For example, changing the time that Bob's food-grabbing social story is presented, from just before lunch to earlier in the morning, may allow him to reflect on appropriate behaviors and thus improve the program. On the other hand, if the time and the story content were changed at the same time, the teacher would be unsure of which factor was responsible for Bob's behavior change.

10. **Program for maintenance and generalization.**

After a behavior change has become consistent, the educator may want to fade use of the social story. Fading may be accomplished by extending the time between readings or having students be responsible for reading the story themselves. By their very nature social stories permit generalization across environments. Thus, teachers should assist students in applying social story content to various situations. For example, the teacher could assist Bob in using his appropriate eating skills during snack time, at parties, and in restaurants. In addition, the teacher should ensure that the student continues the appropriate behavior. Finally, students with sufficient independent skills may be assisted in identifying social goals for which they may develop their own social stories.

Note. Adapted from "Using Social Stories to Teach Social and Behaviorial Skills to Children with Autism," by B. L. Swaggart et al., 1995, *Focus on Autistic Behavior, 10*(1), 1–16. Copyright 1995 by PRO-ED, Inc.; and from "Implementing Cognitive Behavior Management Programs for Persons with Autism: Guidelines for Practitioners," by C. Quinn, B. L. Swaggart, and B. S. Myles, 1994, *Focus on Autistic Behavior, 9*(4), 1–13. Copyright 1994 by PRO-ED, Inc. Adapted with permission.

Social Scripts

Children and youth with Asperger Syndrome may also benefit from having adults structure their behaviors through the use of scripts. For instance, a child and his teacher may practice a script for joining in a group game at recess. This option minimizes problems these children have with being able to spontaneously generate language and deal with the complexity of deciding how to approach peers. Moreover, when paired with peer interaction training (i.e., direct instruction and adult- and peer-mediated strategies), it provides a structured interactive routine that facilitates predictable responses.

There is no question that scripting social interactions has severe limitations in producing high-quality, naturalistic interactions. That is, it is difficult to script interactions, and when scripts are used they tend to result in somewhat stilted, pedantic, and clumsy responses. Nevertheless, social scripts can be effectively used to structure initial appropriate initiations (e.g., statements for engaging or connecting with other students) by a learner with Asperger Syndrome. Furthermore, this strategy tends to be most effective in combination with peer training. That is, peers who are engaged in interactions based on social scripting require information regarding how to respond and strategies for moving conversations and interactions beyond initial social scripts.

Acting Lessons

Citing their personal experience, many adults with Asperger Syndrome suggest that acting lessons are an appropriate means of teaching children and youth about social and emotional issues to aid in self-awareness, self-calming, and self-management. During acting lessons, children learn to express, verbally and nonverbally, emotions in specific situations. They also learn to interpret others' emotions, feelings, and voices. Perhaps more important, acting class participants engage in simulations and receive feedback from an instructor and peers regarding their performance.

Self-Esteem Building

The child or youth with Asperger Syndrome may look different, act different, feel different (and, in some ways, *be* different) from other people. The child often knows this, and loss of self-esteem is often the by-product. Especially as adults, there is a high price to pay for negative self-esteem. It has been documented that adults with Asperger Syndrome have higher levels of depression, suicide, and other affective disorders than the general population, which can be partially related to self-concept problems (Williams, 2001).

Educators and parents need to work together to help the child understand that she is more than the exceptionality. She is not Asperger Syndrome. She is a child who has this exceptionality, but this is only one part of her. She has many other characteristics that should be pointed out and celebrated (Bieber, 1994). In fact, aspects other than the disorder should be the primary focus in order to prevent the exceptionality from receiving so much attention and making it the major facet of the child's identity.

The child needs assistance in developing a positive self-image. This is built, in part, by successful experiences. LaVoie (cited in Bieber, 1994) poignantly challenges teachers and parents to find the "island of competence" in the child, to stress it and celebrate it. Presenting multiple opportunities for the child to demonstrate her "island of competence" builds self-esteem.

Strategies to build self-esteem include the following:

- Place the child in the role of helper or tutor.

- Tell the child what she is doing right; reframe negative language to positive language.

- Determine what the child does well and help her do more of it.

- Compliment the child and teach her to compliment herself.

The Power Card

The Power Card is a visual aid that builds on a child's special interest to teach appropriate social interactions, behavior expectations, the meaning of language, and the hidden curriculum. A scenario is created around an individual associated with the child's special interest and the behavior or situation that needs to be addressed. Written at the individual's comprehension level, the scenario may contain pictures or graphics related to the special interest. The individual associated with the special interest then attempts a solution to the problem. The child is then encouraged to try out the appropriate behavior, which is written in a series of short steps. A Power Card, the size of a bookmark, business card, or trading card, is then designed for the child to carry. The Power Card contains the short series of steps and a picture of the special interest (Gagnon, 2001).

For example, Mark is a highly intelligent sixth-grade student with Asperger Syndrome. He hopes to attend Harvard and speaks of this often to anyone willing to listen. He begins many sentences with, "When I go to Harvard. . . ." Even though Mark is an excellent student, he struggles socially and finds that he has little in common with other children his age. Despite a desire to have friends, he is not quite sure what to do. His interactions typically consist of bragging about his academic skills and referring to those who are not quite as bright as "peasants." He also has difficulty understanding humor and tends to laugh inappropriately and loudly. The following scenario and the Power Card shown in Figure 5.1 were introduced to Mark to address his tendency to brag and laugh loudly and inappropriately.

▶ Using the Power Card To Teach Appropriate Interactions

Dave is proud to be a student at Harvard. He spent many hours studying in middle school and high school so that he could achieve his dream. He spent so much time studying that he had little time for other things. When he found out that he was accepted to Harvard, he spent a lot of time bragging to others in his high school class and laughing loudly about his accomplishment. No one wanted to talk to him about Harvard, but Dave just told himself that they were jealous of his accomplishments.

When Dave got to Harvard, he realized that he wanted to have friends, but he continued his bragging behavior. He also continued to laugh too loudly and at inappropriate times. Dave scheduled a meeting with his English professor and explained his problems to him. The professor gave him the following advice:

1. Don't brag about yourself. Others will like you more if they have a chance to discover how wonderful you are on their own.

2. You can tell when to laugh by laughing when others laugh. If you are unsure about laughing, it is better to just smile.

3. If everyone in a group is laughing, try to blend your laughter with theirs.

Mark, you do not have to wait to get to Harvard to practice these three things. Dave now knows that he would have enjoyed middle and high school much more if he had tried these things when he was younger.

> **POWER CARD**
>
> **To be successful at Harvard,
> it is important to remember:**
>
> 1. Don't brag.
> 2. Laugh only when others laugh.
> 3. Try to blend your laughter.

Figure 5.1. Sample Power Card. (The card should be about the size of a trading card.)

Strategies for Positive Social Peer Contacts

Planning for positive social peer contacts requires professionals and parents to (a) identify and arrange appropriate social interaction opportunities, (b) teach students with Asperger Syndrome and their nondisabled peers the knowledge and skills needed to take advantage of social interaction opportunities, and (c) ensure that students with Asperger Syndrome and their peers receive benefit and reinforcement for their social interaction efforts. An example of an appropriate and mutually beneficial peer social interaction program is shown in Table 5.3.

Adult-Mediated Strategies

In this context, "adult mediated" refers to social skill and social interactions that are directly orchestrated and structured by teachers, paraeducators, parents, or other adults. Adult-mediated strategies involve two basic procedures. First, the child or youth with Asperger Syndrome is paired with a socially desirable peer in a setting supportive of social interaction. In this context, "socially desirable" refers to a child who is willing and able to follow

Table 5.3
Positive Social Peer Interaction Program

1. **Identify and arrange for appropriate social interaction opportunities.**

   Leroy, a third-grade student with Asperger Syndrome, has recently become disruptive during recess. Leroy will dash into a kickball game or other group activity in which he is not a participant, grab the ball, and race away. Various intervention attempts, including loss of recess, have proved to be unsuccessful. A functional analysis related to this problem revealed that Leroy appears to have few appropriate strategies for gaining his classmates' attention. As a result, Leroy's teacher has begun to develop a plan for improving his recess behavior, especially related to providing instruction and support that will allow this student more appropriate ways of being involved with and engaging in age-suitable social interactions with peers.

2. **Teach students with Asperger Syndrome and their nondisabled peers the knowledge and skills needed to take advantage of social interaction opportunities.**

   Leroy and his third-grade teacher have been regularly discussing appropriate recess behavior and practicing ways to appropriately interact and play with peers. Leroy's teacher also presented to his entire class a unit on persons with disabilities, including those with Asperger Syndrome.

3. **Ensure that students with Asperger Syndrome and their peers receive benefit and reinforcement for their social interaction efforts.**

   After undergoing training with his teacher, Leroy was invited to select three peers to play a game with at recess. Prior to that session, Leroy's teacher reviewed and practiced with him the targeted game and social skills that he had previously been instructed to use. Following a successful recess experience with peers, Leroy and his peers received social praise and additional free time following work completion. Leroy's teacher also continued to monitor her student for appropriate recess behavior.

---

directions, engage in desired social behaviors, and model appropriate social responses. The identified peer (or peers) is instructed to remain close to the child with Asperger Syndrome during specified times such as recess, free time, and so forth. The peer is also instructed to be prepared to participate in a game or activity with the child if the child initiates or otherwise indicates interest in engaging in social interaction.

Second, to facilitate social interactions between the child with Asperger Syndrome and the designated peer, an adult (e.g., classroom teacher, school paraprofessional) remains close to the child and provides verbal prompts. For instance, a teacher may prompt a child to approach a peer who has been coached to be receptive to playing a game or sharing an activity. If the child with Asperger Syndrome complies with the prompt, his or her behavior is reinforced by the adult. If the child fails to follow the adult's prompt, the directive is repeated, and when appropriate the adult physically assists the child in following the prompt. An example of an adult-mediated strategy follows.

▶ Adult-Mediated Instruction of a Free-Period Activity

During free periods, Ms. Rodriguez, a third-grade teacher, notices that Angela is not engaged in an activity. Ms. Rodriguez prompts Angela to ask another student to participate in an activity such as playing a computer game. Following this prompt, Angela approaches a peer and asks if she would like to play Family Feud on the computer. The peer agrees to play a computer game; however, she indicates a desire to play a different game. In response, Ms. Rodriguez prompts Angela to offer a list of choices to her peer. When the students mutually agree on a computer game and begin to play, the teacher stays close by. Ms. Rodriguez praises Angela for her playing techniques and prompts her as needed.

There is little doubt that adult-mediated social interaction programs can be effective. Adult-mediated strategies can be (a) used to develop a variety of social skills in a variety of settings, (b) used with groups of children, and (c) generalized through careful planning. Disadvantages of adult-mediated strategies should also be considered when planning social interaction programs. The most distinct disadvantage is that adult-mediated strategies may disrupt natural and ongoing peer social exchanges. That is, the presence of an adult in an ongoing peer exchange is unnatural and may interfere with reciprocal interactions. For instance, a child with Asperger Syndrome may continually seek support and guidance from an adult and respond only when prompted. Moreover, when the child with Asperger Syndrome does respond, the adult mediation may further the development of stiff, unnatural interactions. In spite of these potential problems, adult-mediated strategies have been found to be among the most effective ways of increasing social interactions.

Peer-Mediated Strategies

Peer-mediated strategies involve socially competent peers who are taught to initiate and support social interactions with children and youth with Asperger Syndrome. Following such training, these individuals are placed in social situations where they participate in social activities with the children and youth with Asperger Syndrome. Unlike adult-mediated strategies, no adults provide social interaction prompts. Rather, after training, children with Asperger Syndrome and their peers participate in social activities independent of direct adult involvement.

This strategy has been associated with an increase in positive, appropriate behaviors by individuals with disabilities, which in turn promotes peer acceptance. There is some indication that peer-mediated strategies are most effective when popular, high-status peers serve as confederates. Use of groups composed of two peers and one child with Asperger Syndrome has also been advocated by some researchers as a means of obtaining higher levels of social interaction and promoting more normal social interaction patterns. An example of a peer-mediated strategy follows.

▶ Peer-Mediated Activity

Miss Simmons decides to adopt a peer-mediated strategy to increase social interactions between Latanya and her classmates. This decision is based on Miss Simmons's observation that Latanya is consistently isolated from her peers during recess, free time, and lunch periods. Prior to selecting an appropriate peer, Miss Simmons identifies a classmate who occasionally talks to and plays with Latanya. Miss Simmons invites the peer to participate in a social interaction enhancement program. Upon the peer's acceptance, Miss Simmons trains Latanya and the peer to interact during a variety of activities, including how the peer should respond to Latanya's invitations to play, prompting procedures, and reinforcement methods. Subsequent to peer training, Miss Simmons observes the students, makes suggestions, and offers feedback as needed. However, during the social activity itself, she allows Latanya and her peer to interact independently .

There are a number of advantages to using peer-mediated strategies. First, this approach is the most natural means of promoting socialization because it relies on naturally occurring interactions between peers. After initial training, adults permit children to socialize, thus ensuring that activities are based on normally occurring social interactions and on behaviors of socially competent peers rather than on artificial or simulated scenarios. Peer-mediated strategies are relatively easy to implement and typically offer the best results in terms of quantity and quality of social interaction.

Weaknesses of peer-mediated strategies include the question of whether social interaction skills will be generalized to other peers, environments, and situations, because the children are trained to work with designated peers in their classroom on certain activities. There is also a question of whether skills developed by children through peer-mediated strategies will be maintained over time. Thus, generalization and maintenance programs must be planned.

Interpretation

Even when the person with Asperger Syndrome receives effective instruction in the social and behavioral realms, situations will occur that require interpretation. A number of interpretive strategies can help turn seemingly random actions into meaningful interactions for individuals with Asperger Syndrome. These include (a) cartooning, (b) social autopsies, and (c) the Situation Options Consequences Choices Strategies Simulation strategy.

Cartooning

Visual symbols such as cartooning have been found to enhance the processing abilities of persons in the autism spectrum and to enhance their understanding of the environment (Hagiwara & Myles, 1999; Kuttler, Myles, & Carlson, 1998). One type of visual support is cartooning. The technique has been implemented by speech–language pathologists for years to enhance understanding in their clients. Cartoon figures play an integral role in a number of intervention techniques: pragmaticism (Arwood, 1991), mind reading (Howlin et al., 1999), and comic strip conversations (Gray, 1995).

Comic strip conversations were introduced by Gray (1995) to illustrate and interpret social situations and provide support to "students who struggle to comprehend the quick exchange of information which occurs in a conversation" (p. 2). Comic strip conversations promote social understanding by incorporating simple figures and other symbols in a comic strip format. Speech, thought bubble symbols, and color are used to help the individual with Asperger Syndrome see and analyze a conversation. According to Attwood (1998), comic strip conversations "allow the child to analyze and understand the range of messages and meanings that are a natural part of conversation and play. Many children with Asperger Syndrome are confused and upset by teasing or sarcasm. The speech and thought bubble as well as choice of colors can illustrate the hidden messages" (p. 72). Educators can draw a social situation to facilitate understanding or assist the student in doing his or her own illustrations.

Effectiveness of cartooning has limited scientific verification (Rogers & Myles, 2001). Nonetheless, there is mounting clinical evidence that some students with Asperger Syndrome are good candidates for social learning based on adults' use of a comic format to dissect and interpret social situations and interactions. That is, in a fashion similar to the way in which comic strips are designed, a social situation can be analyzed in step-by-step fashion with an individual, including an attempt to speculate about the motives, interpretations, and social responses of others.

For example, Tom, an eighth-grade student with Asperger Syndrome, often had difficulty understanding the intentions of others. He was particularly concerned about what girls said about him, reporting that they "made fun of him." Tom's teacher used a cartoon format to illustrate an incident that caused Tom a great deal of anxiety. Specifically, Tom was troubled because a girl told him he had a "cute butt." The girl was attempting to tell Tom that she liked him, but Tom perceived the comment as sexual harassment and told the girl that she was a sexist pig. Figure 5.2 contains a comic strip that Tom's teacher used with him to interpret the situation.

Figure 5.2. Sample comic strip conversation. *Note.* From "Using Social Stories and Comic Strip Conversations To Interpret Social Situations for an Adolescent with Asperger Syndrome," by M. F. Rogers and B. S. Myles, 2001, *Intervention in School and Clinic, 36,* p. 312. Copyright 2001 by PRO-ED, Inc. Reprinted with permission.

Situation Options Consequences Choices Strategies Simulation

The Situation Options Consequences Choices Strategies Simulation (SOCCSS) strategy was developed to help students with social interaction problems put interpersonal relationships into a sequential form (J. Roosa, personal communication, June 4, 1997). It helps students understand problem situations and lets them see that they have to make choices about a given situation, with each choice having a consequence. The SOCCSS strategy works as follows:

1. *Situation*. When a social problem arises, the teacher works with the student to identify the situation. Specifically, they identify (a) who was involved; (b) what happened; (c) the date, day, and time of occurrence; and (d) reasons for the present situation. Together they define the problem and state a goal through discussion, writing, and drawings.

2. *Options*. Following identification of the situation, the student and teacher brainstorm several options for the identified behavior. At this point, the teacher accepts all student responses and does not evaluate them. Typically, the options are listed in written or pictorial format. According to Spivack, Platt, and Shure (1976), this step is critical to problem solving. The ability to generate multiple solutions diminishes student frustration, encourages the student to see more than one perspective, and results in student resiliency.

3. *Consequences*. Together the student and teacher evaluate each of the options generated. Kaplan and Carter (1995) suggested that the options be evaluated for (a) efficacy (Will the solution get me what I want?) and (b) feasibility (Will I be able to do it?). Each of the consequences is labeled with an E for efficacy or F for feasibility. For younger children, the options can be labeled as plus (+) for acceptable or minus (–) for unacceptable, ordered on a rating scale, or identified by happy or sad faces. The teacher works as a facilitator, helping the student to develop consequences for each option without dictating the consequences. The teacher uses pointed questions to help the student develop his or her own consequences.

4. *Choices*. During this stage, with the assistance of an adult as needed, the student selects the option or options that will have the most desirable consequences.

5. *Strategies*. A planned action is developed by the student and teacher. The plan should be generated by the student to facilitate ownership. The teacher should ask questions that lead the student into developing an effective plan.

6. *Simulation*. Finally, the student is given an opportunity to role-play the solution. In the simulation phase the student might do the following: (a) find a quiet place to image how the strategy will work, (b) talk with a peer about the plan of action, (c) write down on paper what may

occur when the strategy is implemented, and (d) practice or role-play with one or more people the strategy developed to address the problem.

Figure 5.3 is an example of a worksheet that can be used to facilitate SOCCSS.

Social Autopsies

Social autopsies were developed by Richard LaVoie (Bieber, 1994) to help students with severe learning and social problems develop an understanding of social mistakes. An autopsy, in the traditional sense, is the examination and inspection of a dead body to discover the cause of death, determine damage, and prevent occurrence of the cause of death in others. A social autopsy is an examination and inspection of a social error to discover the cause of the error, determine the damage, and prevent it from occurring again. When a social mistake occurs, the student meets with an educator or caregiver to discuss it. Together, in a nonpunitive fashion, they identify the mistake. They then discuss who was harmed by the error. The third step of the autopsy is development of a plan to ensure that the error does not occur again. Because of the visual strengths, problem-solving deficits, and language-processing problems of children with Asperger Syndrome, social autopsies may be enhanced by using written words or phrases or pictures to illustrate each of the steps.

Concluding Thoughts

Without question, children and youth with Asperger Syndrome benefit from social interaction training. However, different children have different needs, and different situations call for different programs. Thus, it is likely that social interaction programs will prove to be useful at least with certain individuals and in certain situations. The success of social interaction programs may be enhanced by careful consideration of several factors:

• Adults associated with children and youth with Asperger Syndrome must carefully and collaboratively establish appropriate social interaction goals. It is not appropriate or reasonable to expect that

SOCCSS WORKSHEET

Situation	
Who	What
When	Why

Options	Consequences	Choices

Strategies

Simulation Type	Simulation Outcomes

Follow-up

Figure 5.3. SOCCSS worksheet. *Note.* Adapted from "Understanding the Hidden Curriculum: An Essential Social Skill for Children and Youth with Asperger Syndrome," by B. S. Myles and R. L. Simpson, 2001, *Intervention in School and Clinic*, *36*(5), p. 284. Copyright 2001 by PRO-ED, Inc. Adapted with permission. Originally adapted from *Men on the Move: Competence and Cooperation "Conflict Resolution and Beyond,"* by J. B. Roosa, 1995, Kansas City, MO: Author.

these children will become socially skilled and sophisticated as a result of any intervention program Although reasonable improvements can be expected, it is highly unlikely that the strategies discussed in this section will produce a "cure."

- Adults involved in designing and implementing social interaction programs for children and youth with Asperger Syndrome should design their programs to coincide with existing social interaction activities and opportunities, as opposed to creating entirely new situations.
- Social interaction programs should be designed to allow for the fact that these programs require both initial and ongoing training and support. It is unreasonable to expect that once a program is initiated, it will effectively continue without ongoing support.
- Social interaction programs should include plans for skill generalization and maintenance.

There is little question that children and youth with Asperger Syndrome present significant social and behavioral challenges for professionals and parents and require a variety of supports. However, when given appropriate structure, social interaction opportunities, and behavior management support, they can be expected to demonstrate skill and progress.

Understanding the Impact of Asperger Syndrome on the Family

6

Parents and families of individuals with Asperger Syndrome contend with a variety of challenges for which they have little or no training. As with parents and families of individuals with any disability, they experience anger, disappointment, frustration, and a variety of other emotions related directly or indirectly to the disorder. At the same time, however, they are expected to understand and support their family member with Asperger Syndrome without the benefit of widespread information about the condition and with little public understanding of it. Hence, in addition to having to deal with significant personal challenges with little or no support, these families often must educate others about the mysteries, characteristics, and challenges associated with Asperger Syndrome.

For these reasons the voices and reflections of parents and family members of individuals with Asperger Syndrome comprise this chapter. Our hope, and the hope of those who have contributed to this chapter, is that their experiences will benefit other parents and families as well as professionals who work with individuals with Asperger Syndrome.

Michelle

Michelle is a teenager with Asperger Syndrome. Her diagnosis was made when she was 12 years old. Before then, Michelle's odd, stubborn, detached nature was a mystery, as were the means to help her.

Michelle was always a "difficult" child whose dogged adherence to her own unique way of doing things made life difficult for her and those around her. Even her birth was difficult and unique, in that she was delivered faceup (the reverse of the norm). This might have been endearing, but as with so much of Michelle's subsequent "uniqueness," the effect was unnecessary travail. In this case, faceup meant 23 hours of painful labor for Mom.

Michelle was not an easy infant to love. She showed displeasure regularly and effectively by uncontrolled, unrelenting screaming. This was especially so on occasions marked by change. A car trip at 3 months, for example, meant ceaseless wailing on the road. The only peace came with sleep, and that was unpredictable and scarce. Hotel rooms, relatives' homes—any strange environment—were met in a similar way. Eventually, Mom and Dad resigned themselves to the idea that this was just "colic," even though it didn't always fit what the book said, especially the part about "gone in 3 months" (6 or 8 was more like it!).

As an infant, Michelle was always a bit stiff and squirmy when held. She never cuddled, and she resisted physical closeness and affection. Although she could be engaged socially in play and enjoyed silliness, she was not inclined to interact with others and preferred playing by herself. Near the end of the first year, she began to demonstrate a faraway look when in the company of other children. A photo of her first birthday party is typical—four other little girls are all focused on some minor event, while Michelle has a trancelike expression, her thoughts focused elsewhere. Then, as now, Michelle was rarely "in the moment." She is barely aware of people, objects, or events happening now. Her mind is elsewhere—actively thinking—but not here, not now.

Socially, Michelle the toddler was much the same. Her mom made repeated efforts to foster friendships by inviting little girls to play, but things seldom "clicked." Usually, Michelle seemed disinterested. Even when Michelle tried to interact with others, her efforts were awkward and ineffective. At about this same time, though, Michelle did find a friend, a neighbor girl named Tamika. Tamika was quite slow and almost as unusual in her behavior as Michelle (e.g., Tamika, who was supremely self-assured, unself-consciously kept a pacifier in her mouth most of the time, well into her 5th year!).

The two girls were almost constant companions from the age of 1 until 6 years, when Tamika and her family moved. Each seemed oblivious to the oddities of the other. And although their personalities did not "mesh," they succeeded as friends by adopting a "parallel" style of play, each doing her own thing, but "together." This style persisted until Tamika moved, well past the age when parallel play is considered "normal."

At age 2, Michelle got a baby brother. Although Brother assumed secondary importance to friend Tamika, he was nonetheless a close companion, whose acceptance of Michelle was total. Michelle, for her part, took a protective role toward her baby brother.

At age 4, Michelle was enrolled in preschool 3 days per week. Her parents, convinced that she was very bright, were shocked at the negative reports from her teachers. They were concerned that Michelle did not interact well with the other children—very concerned. About the same time, Michelle developed an odd attachment to a tree by the house. An old scrub oak in the back yard inexplicably became "her" tree, a fond attachment that was mentioned several times a year and lasted almost a decade. Her affection was demonstrated by long periods spent at the base of the tree and by excited, animated remarks about the tree, Michelle's "old friend."

Grade school was an interesting time. Standard IQ testing conducted with all of the kindergarten students indicated that Michelle had a full-scale IQ of 130. Nevertheless, her teacher, an older woman with a definite authoritarian bent, was unhappy with Michelle's work and behavior. She seldom made appreciative remarks about Michelle to her parents. Instead, she often seemed disgusted with Michelle, and Michelle often appeared sad and frustrated. Not surprisingly, the teacher recommended that Michelle repeat kindergarten.

Michelle was lucky to get a new and very different kindergarten teacher the second time around. The teacher obviously liked Michelle and had an appreciation for her unique ways. This teacher, in fact, appeared to like all children, seemed happy and secure about herself, and was not hung up on authority. This was a perfect recipe for Michelle, and it produced a happier, more contented student.

Over the years, this teacher model worked well for Michelle on many occasions. Stern, authoritarian teachers, even though beneficial for many students, were bad for Michelle. Michelle was never able to please the regimentarian, whose emphasis on order and punctuality was largely beyond Michelle's grasp. Teachers like this could be counted on to have a bad effect both on her performance and on her behavior, and especially on how she felt about herself.

It was fortunate that the ensuing 4 years of school brought a succession of reasonably accepting, supportive teachers who allowed Michelle to be herself. They usually found her interesting and engaging, in her own unique way. They were realistic about her progress but nonetheless were careful not to be overcritical of her spotty schoolwork and inattentiveness in class. Although Michelle was by no means an ideal student, she was compliant and never disruptive.

Michelle's behavior around other children continued to be unusual in grade school. Described as aloof, unattached, and a lone wolf, Michelle rarely interacted with other kids at school unless as part of a group game directed by the teacher. During free times in recess, Michelle would typically wander about by herself, happily engrossed in her own thoughts. The main exception to this pattern—and it happened regularly—was that she would often seek out adults for "conversation." The conversation was usually one-sided, with Michelle rambling on in a somewhat pedantic fashion about some topic of her choosing. Out of politeness and a certain degree of interest, teachers allowed this but would eventually break it off to discourage monopolizing by Michelle and to encourage her to mix with other kids.

Home life for Michelle during most of grade school followed the pattern set earlier. Friendship with Tamika remained the same as before until Tamika moved. Despite the central and important role that Tamika had played, her parting, although duly noted on many occasions, was not met with any overt sadness or sense of loss. Attempts to foster interaction with "normal" girls continued to be unsuccessful but were seemingly more painful for Michelle's parents than for Michelle.

A move to a different neighborhood around age 8 brought a new selection of potential playmates for Michelle, but there was no improvement. One interesting relationship did develop out of the move, however. Michelle came to revere a pretty and rather snobbish little girl next door and made overtures of friendship. A relationship did develop, because of Michelle's obvious high regard for the neighbor and the neighbor's esteem for anyone who recognized how wonderful she was. After several months, however, the relationship grew tiresome for the neighbor, who abruptly ended it.

Michelle, unfazed and unashamed, made repeated, earnest, although awkward efforts to regain the friend. After several failures, she hit on something that worked—she became the neighbor's servant, performing all sorts of tasks in return for the attentions of the "friend." Even when this unusual arrangement lost its appeal for the neighbor, Michelle accepted this second loss of the friend without remorse or humiliation. Unfortunately, this detached attitude toward humiliation was not to last forever.

At home, grade-schooler Michelle spent a great deal of her time alone in her room. Although there was a brief interest in stamp collecting, most of her activities seemed pointless. She had difficulty maintaining attention to any particular activity and thus would rapidly pass from one activity to another, never completing anything. Dad made a fairly regular habit of reading to Michelle in her room, especially *Highlights* magazine, which gave mutual delight. Michelle liked doing homework with Dad at this stage, especially when Dad presented the material verbally. It was also at this stage that Michelle's extreme inherent messiness became apparent in her room, at the table, and particularly at school, where her disorganization was always duly noted by the teacher.

Michelle obviously did not want to be messy and disorganized, and she was never hostile at attempts by others to help her "shape up." She simply was incapable of sustaining organization. It is likely that her inattention to the "here and now" made neatness seem unimportant. Organization may also have demanded too dear a price, requiring as it does a sustained marshaling of attention, which for Michelle was very tedious, tiring, and even exhausting.

Grade 5 marked a significant change at school. Not only did the difficulty of the work increase at this time, but the teacher also departed from his predecessors' laissez-faire attitude. Instead, he demanded conformity in schoolwork and was unwilling to be flexible about this. Despite her native intelligence, Michelle was generally unable to cope with the demands of finishing work and turning it in of her own accord, not to mention keeping track of homework assignments and so on. Efforts on the part of her parents to modify teacher demands in light of Michelle's short-comings were not successful. It was the teacher's belief that developing organizational ability and responsibility came first. Any child could do it, if he or she would only will it. This remained the predominant refrain of Michelle's teachers for the next 4 years, resulting in Michelle's not improving noticeably in responsibility or organization, as well as learning very little.

The rigidity of the fifth-grade teacher was repeated by the sixth-grade teacher, only much more so. Although dynamic and effective with most of her class, this teacher was unable to accept nonconformity in a student, or messiness, or disorganization, or any of the many traits that flow out of these three. This teacher could make the trains run on time, but she was unconcerned about those who were left at the station, usually Michelle. In fact, Michelle's nonconformity eventually made the teacher dislike her.

At the same time that Michelle's teachers were becoming convinced of her unworthiness, Michelle was reaching the same conclusion on her own. In early adolescence, Michelle was experiencing the same growth of self-awareness that most kids do. Although for most kids this process is positive, in Michelle's case it was not. Up until then, the fact that Michelle was a loner who was unable to "connect" with other children and be part of the group had been of little concern to her. She was content to spend recess and lunch virtually alone and was unconcerned about her lack of friends.

Once self-awareness developed, however, Michelle's realization that she did not fit in was very painful. As a result, she became depressed, and her cheerful demeanor changed to one of sadness, frustration, and even anger. At home she stayed in her room almost exclusively. To relieve stress, she began the distressing habit of cutting on herself with a pin or small knife. Although the cuts were superficial and not dangerous, they were obvious enough to send shock waves throughout the school and family. It was clear to those who knew her well that the cutting was not intended to produce harm, but to relieve stress; however, "caring" adults at school and elsewhere were anxious about it. Questions about suicide naturally followed. "Yes," she sometimes thought about dying. "Yes," she had thought about suicide. As you might imagine, this was all it took to unleash a flood of attention. Michelle, who was suffering from an inability to connect and to engage others in conversation, had found a means to be important, to avoid being ignored.

What followed was not good. Michelle not only received endless attention from adults and kids alike for disquieting remarks, but also quickly learned the game and became very good at it. Manipulation did not enter into Michelle's intentions, though. To Michelle she was simply getting what she needed in the best way she knew. Of course, any child could be seduced by this sort of instant attention. Whereas most early adolescents sense the cost and avoid talking about suicide entirely, or else give it up fairly rapidly, Michelle did not understand, and so she persisted. Once this suicide material lost its impact, it was replaced with other shocking things. Unfortunately, Michelle could not comprehend the negative impact it was having on peers, for whom the sense of her oddness and undesirability was only strengthened.

This behavior eventually led to the psychologist's office, where the downward spiral continued. In an effort to uncover any underlying psychopathology, the psychologist encouraged Michelle to express any morbid or horrible thoughts that might be lurking in the dark recesses of her mind. Michelle, for her part, was most willing to oblige. In time she produced loads of shocking fantasies for the doctor, who, in exchange, provided Michelle with lots of high-quality, satisfying attention.

Both doctor and patient were duped. For the psychologist, the result was a wildly mistaken diagnosis of extremely morbid personality. For Michelle, the attention merely reinforced the notion that shocking remarks work. Michelle's remarks about cutting and suicide became even more common, supplanted in time by fictitious musings about her lesbianism, multiple personalities, and criminal friends.

Brent

Santa Claus was preparing to visit the preschool our son attended. It was time to question the children singly about the Christmas presents they hoped to get. Suddenly, our boy pulled Santa's chair away, and jolly old St. Nick went down in a heap. The other children and their parents didn't know what to make of it. Neither did my wife or I.

More than 8 years were to pass before we received a diagnosis of Asperger Syndrome, often called high-functioning autism. The diagnosis would at least place in clearer focus the preschool embarrassment and over a dozen other examples of our son's quirkiness.

Although Santa has reportedly recovered, Mom and Dad are worn slick dealing with pediatricians, psychiatrists, psychologists, allergists, pharmacologists, therapists, educational consultants, and counselors—not to leave out medical insurers, public and private school personnel, and home schoolers. Oh, yes—we also moved 900 miles to a presumably allergy-friendly environment (where new allergies replaced old ones) and within a couple of months moved right back to accommodate homesickness. We were prepared to go to any length.

The Asperger diagnosis, however late, now helps lessen what must be called "parental panic." We're sharper about what to expect, about how we should deal with it, about being ready to cope with the unexpected. One might reasonably ask whether such a diagnosis also brings apprehensions about our son's future—about his prospects for navigating successfully the maze of social rituals, the most stressful of all dark places people with Asperger Syndrome must enter. Yes, the diagnosis has brought new worries, particularly about his impending adolescent dating and whether he will understand fully the commitment required for marriage, for child rearing, for productive work relationships. There's also the worry about which Asperger traits he might pass to his children.

And yet—even with all the day-to-day adjustments for us, as well as those future uncertainties—there's an unexpected "up" side. More on that in a moment.

The Asperger Syndrome diagnosis and our subsequent examination of the literature has helped us understand much that has haunted us for years, questions such as

- Why, when he was a toddler and able to speak clearly, did our son respond with only a vacant stare to our cheery greetings?

- Why did he resist hugs, yet during naps with Mom or Dad seem to glue the full length of his body to our backs?

- Why did he throw himself to the floor and scream when anyone turned on a vacuum cleaner?

- Why were his questions becoming more and more repetitious, as though he'd never heard our answers?

- Why, through most of his boyhood, couldn't our son catch a ball one-to-one with Dad or learn to throw it accurately?

- When a classmate's dog died and our son learned of it, why did our boy react by laughing in the bereaved youngster's face?

- Why after play experiences that brought resentful howls from teammates did our son insist that he'd only wished to help the other side?

- Why in his earlier school years did he become terribly disoriented when having to shift to new tasks?

- Where did all those on-again, off-again tics come from— and the odd hand and arm movements, incessant coughing, stuttering, loud nose blowing?

- What triggers those periodic and frightening anxiety attacks, at times marked by vigorous self-biting and hand banging?

- Why do "friends" abandon him with such heartbreaking consistency?

- Why for so long was he uncomfortable in pants snug at the waist and intent on wearing inappropriate but softer sweat clothes?

- When our son is being introduced to individuals, why does his body stiffen and his face assume a startled expression— even though he can address a roomful of people with relative ease?

- How is it possible for him to play the piano with near perfection for an audience when the performance follows unsteady practice sessions that frequently end in emotional breakdowns?

- Why are his reading comprehension scores declining alarmingly?

- When furnished with a wide range of reading material at an early age, why did he immerse himself instead in promotional books from automobile showrooms?

- What accounts for the near-zero motivation and low energy level in a youngster of such high intelligence?

- What makes our son convert a simple apology into a kind of persevering self-flagellation—to a point that used to drive Mom and Dad to distraction?

Where there were only guesses before there are now answers—though of limited satisfaction—to all these questions in the context of Asperger Syndrome. Notice also from the varying tenses that there's been a movement forward in our son's ability to shift tasks, catch a ball, dress more appropriately. There's also been progress in terms of his parents' enlarged capacity for patient understanding and growing conviction that some Asperger traits can be short-circuited, if not overcome.

Although doctors can judge where the combinations of behavior might place a child on the continuum of autism, they're far from knowing why children with Asperger Syndrome manifest these behaviors. There is also little consensus on whether the most distressing Asperger symptoms can truly be changed, whether by behavior modification or through biochemistry.

We parents, on whom medical practitioners depend for answers to a greater extent than we might have expected, are pretty much at the same stage as those who first tried to invent the wheel. Parents must first examine every clue to what might benefit or in some way comfort their children, try it, try it again, and, failing in that approach, back off and try something else.

For example, my 12-year-old son and I attended a conference of the organization More Advanced Autistic People (MAAP). Among the many things I learned was that Asperger children like to be "wrapped" or "cocooned" at times (which helped explain his early-childhood napping position). My son had for months before the conference developed a nightly habit of coughing and twitching 30 to 90 minutes before falling asleep. When he asked (in the motel room on the way back from the conference) whether he could lie down with me, I said, "Sure!" and proceeded to stroke his head slowly, rhythmically, and very gently. He coughed maybe 9 or 10 times and fell asleep within 5 minutes. On subsequent tries of this same method at home, I got it down to less than 2 minutes. At this writing such stroking doesn't seem necessary at all, though we might expect that tic to return. The lesson? He may be growing up and almost as tall as Dad, but there's still a little boy in there—my little boy with special needs.

Those needs now oblige us to know the effects of loud noises on our son and to do everything to avoid them. (Remember the vacuum cleaner?) For instance, unproductive yelling at our younger son, who vexingly has attention-deficit/hyperactivity disorder, has been cut way down. The sensory problems of our son with Asperger Syndrome also involve touch and the way in which various articles of clothing affect or discomfort him.

Conversations and social experiences are being given new attention so that Mom and Dad might discover how to clear the path through what is a terrifying jungle for people with Asperger Syndrome. We now know more about the way our older boy thinks and about the neurologically based differences between how he sees the world and how we do.

We've discovered a few Asperger traits in ourselves, which has helped explain past and present quirks to ourselves and each other. It's given us clues as to how we may help our boy outgrow similar traits that we know served us poorly.

We still find it hard to believe it took so many professionals so many years of sifting through our son's symptoms before two working in concert came up with Asperger Syndrome. Had we known sooner what we know now, we could have averted a number of school crises that have begun to grow more severe in recent years, particularly the way our son's addressing or questioning teachers is customarily perceived by them. He's flippant with teachers—because he has a sense of humor that doesn't take social conventions into account. He may be saying to himself, "I'll try this and see what happens." And when teachers hand out assignments involving six or seven steps and deadlines far in the future, such as a term paper or research project, our boy is overwhelmed. As a sign of wanting to do the right thing about such assignments, he may particularize point by point in order to understand everything expected of him. But it's that questioning that drives teachers up the wall. Seeing that reaction, he decides to run from the task mentally and emotionally. The night before the assignment is due, he may or may not tell Mom or Dad about it and seek help.

Because the label of high-functioning autism now places our son as a public school student under the protection of the Americans with Disabilities Act of 1990, that law is being applied helpfully now. Unlike the experiences of the past, not all teachers are dismissing our boy's quirks by saying things like, "I know when he's pulling my chain." Thanks to the in-house presence of middle school special education professionals, something resembling a coping network is now on alert. We're not saying there's intervention before a crisis such as an anxiety attack. But there is certainly new school staff energy being applied to emergencies involving our son so that those situations don't get worse. We've even noticed a growing preference by the special staff to "work through" the problem at school rather than sending him home. We'd always given him that alternative to ensure he knows there's a safe haven, but maybe their way will be better for him.

Because children with Asperger Syndrome tend to be couch potatoes, given their difficulties in sports, our son was becoming obese. My wife came up with the idea of hiring a personal trainer, who now visits frequently to work out with the boy. Within a very short time, our son started looking better. He seemed also to be feeling better, physically and emotionally. We don't care what this may cost if it works to make our boy healthier and happier.

Earlier I indicated an "up" side to our sudden immersion in the world of Asperger Syndrome and to our learning that our son has this now identifiable, though complicated, disability. We draw optimism from such positives as his abilities in art, music, computers, math, and in memorization, analysis, and special reasoning skills. Where will they lead him? In her book *Thinking in Pictures and Other Reports from My Life with Autism* (1995), Temple Grandin (whom we heard speak at the MAAP conference) makes a good case for the possibility that Albert Einstein may have had what we now call Asperger Syndrome. She names other notables with these traits. Dr. Grandin has high-functioning autism and is a remarkable achiever in animal science. She has designed one third of all livestock-handling facilities currently used in the United States. Just knowing that such a productive life as hers is possible has brightened the outlook for our child.

As parents we're now beyond "Why us?" And because children with Asperger Syndrome show nearly as many differences from one another in symptoms as they do similarities, support group help is limited. Our main focus now is to guide him toward doing his best in every way, while he's still at an age when we can be of maximum influence.

Whenever we look at or listen to this beautiful, talented, heart-of-gold youngster and realize we're lucky enough to be able to say, "He's ours!" we have no doubt about our abilities to meet whatever challenges Asperger Syndrome presents.

Edward

Living with a child with Asperger Syndrome means truly living life one day at a time—frequently 1 minute at a time. Even when the correct diagnosis has finally been reached and you begin to understand where your child's problems come from, living with Asperger Syndrome causes a tremendous amount of frustration and stress for everyone in the family. It affects every aspect of our lives and at times threatens to overwhelm us. But this is our son, so we continue to struggle to make it through one more day.

Each day we are on guard because we never know what situation we may have to deal with. It might be just one of the many misunderstandings that occur so often when Edward is with other people in which we need to intervene to mediate, interpret, or guide him through. It is just as likely that we may have to deal with a situation that is potentially dangerous to himself or others because he doesn't understand cause and effect. As Edward has gotten older, his drastically inappropriate behaviors that occur when he is overstressed have become less frequent but more dangerous. Since there are no warnings to let us know that Edward is becoming stressed, and he is unable to recognize this himself, we all live with at least a slight "fight or flight" response whenever he's around. We must be prepared to take quick, decisive action in situations we would never even have thought of having to deal with. Even though we know that his aggressive and dangerous actions are a stress reaction and not usually related to what is currently going on around him, or aimed at "the victim" personally, it is impossible not to get upset when they occur.

After trying many different medications with only moderate improvement, we have come to the conclusion that the best way to help our son is to decrease his stress level. At home we have done this by taking him off the family chore chart and giving him only one task at a time. We make sure he has "quiet" time in his room at frequent intervals throughout the day and carefully supervise him at all times. Probably the two most important ways we try to decrease his stress at home are to prevent circumstances and situations that are likely to get Edward into trouble and to maintain a strict routine (which frequently means lots of reminding and refocusing of his attention to the task at hand).

Unfortunately, we have not been able to get adequate accommodations outside of home. Since Edward, now in high school, gets good grades when he does the work and doesn't act or look like a person with an obvious disability, there is a refusal to accept the fact that he is handicapped. They choose not to understand that, in spite of his high intelligence, his comprehension of basic life skills, such as right and wrong, self-responsibility, cause and effect, and social obligation and expectations, is similar to that of a child with autism who is cognitively challenged. His ability to perceive, interpret, and respond to other people's cues is also deficient. Since he is unable to filter stimuli, he often withdraws into himself or behaves inappropriately when he's overwhelmed, the same way a child with autism does. They choose not to see that because of these short circuits he will not learn appropriate attitudes and behaviors simply by being around "normal" peers. It's easier for them to think that Edward is intentionally behaving this way or that he's just "odd" and that his inappropriate behavior should simply be ignored.

The result of this "head in the sand" attitude about Edward's disability on the part of the educational system is that we have been forced to watch him struggle on a daily basis with situation after situation that confuses, frustrates, and angers him because he doesn't understand what's going on or the need to do what's expected of him. Because he can't recognize his feelings, he has no way to deal with them, so his stress level builds, causing more and more inappropriate and aggressive behavior. Since all his energy is spent just trying to get through the day at school, he frequently arrives home exhausted and ready to explode from all the stresses and confusions of the day, and the family bears the brunt of it.

In an attempt to try to help him relieve some of this stress, Edward and I have a talk immediately after school each day. We talk about things that are on his mind, good and bad. I try to explain to him why situations went the way they did and to help him put things in perspective. We also use this time for coaching on situations that are likely to occur in the near future, in hopes that this will help him to deal a little better with them and decrease some of his anxiety.

Unfortunately, this doesn't always work, especially if he is angry, stressed, or upset. We have tried to teach him appropriate ways to cope with his feelings, but since he isn't able to recognize what he is feeling, he isn't able to use alternatives when needed. If we encourage him to use them, he becomes very belligerent and angry because he views it as making him do something else he doesn't see a need to do. This only adds to the problem. As Edward becomes more and more stressed, we see a definite increase in random aggression toward his younger brother and sister and, more recently, myself. The aggression takes the form of instigation of activities that are likely to cause the smaller person to get hurt, unnecessary verbal attacks, or physical actions that they can't protect themselves against because he's so much bigger than they are. Even though we have him spending more quiet time in his room at these times, the stress continues to build, and eventually Edward begins to hear voices. He begins to do things that are irrational and potentially dangerous, such as stealing, running away, mixing chemicals or body waste products into drinking or grooming products, experimenting with fire, and many other things most of us would never even think of, much less act on.

Naturally, Edward's problems also affect his younger siblings, Nathaniel and Rosa. It is difficult for them to understand why the big brother they love will suddenly and without apparent cause do or say something that hurts or upsets them. Although most of the time Edward's behaviors are merely annoying or years below his age level, the unpredictability of his behavior has caused his younger siblings to be very wary around him. As Nathaniel, now 8, put it, "I wish I knew if Edward was going to act like my big brother or my little brother so I'd know how to act around him. I can't trust him."

It also puzzles them when Edward continues to repeat inappropriate behaviors that they have long since learned are wrong. Even Rosa, at the young age of 5, recognizes that many of Edward's behaviors and attitudes are "little kid." Since our younger children can't begin to comprehend how someone can quote rules word for word, yet not be able to apply them to himself, we have had to come up with other ways to help them keep their balance of right and wrong. We do things like giving Edward exactly the same consequence for breaking a rule as we do the other two. If the consequence for Nathaniel and Rosa is to stand in the corner for 2 minutes for breaking a certain rule, when Edward breaks that rule, he stands in the corner for 2 minutes. While we older and hopefully wiser folks know that since Edward doesn't connect the consequences with his actions, he is not learning from the situation, we are setting a pattern of consistency for our younger children by letting them know that wrong is wrong no matter who did it, and that the consequence will be the same. It also reassures them to know that Edward's inappropriate actions toward them will be addressed. His handicap is not an excuse for bad behavior.

Another problem area, especially for Nathaniel, is playing with friends. Since Edward's friendships do not continue outside the school setting, he tends to intrude into whatever activity Nathaniel and his friends are doing and to monopolize the situation. The frequent outcome is that Nathaniel winds up getting excluded altogether, which of course makes him angry. The best way we've found to protect Nathaniel's right to have his own friends is to divert Edward into another activity away from the younger kids unless one of us is able to be close by to step in as needed.

Probably the most frequent area of frustration for both siblings is Edward's preference to sit and do nothing or to "zone" (enter the "safety zone" of television or the computer to the exclusion of all else). They enjoy doing things with other people and can't understand that Edward is much more comfortable when he's not interacting with others. After several unsuccessful attempts to get Edward to play with them, they tend to take it personally even though it's not meant that way. Sometimes we allow Edward some "zone" time. Sometimes Mom or Dad steps in and directs Edward and one of the younger children into a physical activity or a mind-challenging game that we keep a constant ear to, just in case intervention becomes necessary.

Probably the easiest thing we do to help minimize the "shutout" feeling Rosa and Nathaniel get from Edward is to encourage them to "snuggle" with him while he's watching television. Although Edward will likely not respond any more than to occasionally put an arm around one of them, he doesn't object when Rosa climbs up on his lap or Nathaniel leans against him, and they feel accepted. It's not unusual to look in the living room in the hour or so before supper and see all three kids snuggled up on the couch watching Nickelodeon. And peace temporarily reigns.

With all the extra time and supervision Edward continues to require from Mom and Dad, the younger children sometimes feel slighted and less important. To try to alleviate some of these feelings, my husband and I have set aside a "story" time at the end of each day for Rosa and Nathaniel. They each have about 10 minutes of guaranteed uninterrupted time with each parent. We may read stories, talk, or maybe play a game. During this time, Edward stays in his room doing an activity of his choice. That way we can give the younger children our undivided attention, reassure them that we love them just as much as their brother, and let them know that they are just as important to us.

In addition to dealing with all of this, as parents of a child with Asperger Syndrome, we are also included in the negative attitude much of the world has about our son. We have been accused of bad parenting, being overly strict, too easy, overprotective, unreasonable, and demanding by educators, parents of our son's peers, and even family members. We often receive disapproving looks when in public because we cannot talk to Edward in the same manner we do our other children if we want him to hear us. While uninformed people's opinions in this area are a relatively minor concern to us, when paired with the fact that we can't leave Edward alone and we can't get sitters to stay with him, our social life is nearly nonexistent. Simply put, if we can't take Edward with us, at least one of us stays home.

Another part of daily life as Edward's parents is exhaustion. Having to be on constant alert and dealing with the 1,001 annoying things Edward does without realizing it takes its toll. Keeping up with a "typical" teenager can be taxing, but providing all the additional supervision Edward needs every day creates a large physical and emotional drain. Unfortunately, nighttime doesn't provide respite either, because Edward frequently can't get to sleep for several hours after he goes to bed, especially when his stress level is up. Knowing the unpredictability of his behavior, we can't sleep until he does. Even then we sleep lightly, always ready to react.

The largest single concern that always lurks in the back of our minds is our son's future. This concern grows daily as Edward approaches adulthood physically and intellectually, while still remaining a very young child in many of the basic skills necessary to be able to survive and succeed in the outside world. We look ahead and see that despite his intelligence, when our son graduates from high school in 2 years, he will not be ready to deal with the demands of college or even a vocational school on his own. The same is true of employment. We don't want to see him forced to sit at home doing nothing because the world will not give him the acceptance, guidance, and accommodation he needs to be a productive member of society.

We also have to think ahead to the time when we are no longer able to provide what he needs. Unfortunately, at this time there is no place for people with Asperger Syndrome to go for assistance of any type, because they fail to meet all criteria to be eligible. This is a frightening concern our family lives with as we try to bring the plight and potential of individuals with Asperger Syndrome to the attention of the public.

Like all families, we have good days and not-so-good days. True, our good days are more stress-filled than the average family's, and our bad days are like living in a war zone, but as in most families, the good days outnumber the bad. We have learned to cherish those infrequent moments when Edward gets all the pieces put together and responds appropriately or with thoughtfulness on his own—moments such as when we walk into a room to find Edward sitting on the couch with a rare expression of peaceful contentment on his face as his two young cousins with autism sleep curled up in his arms. We have also learned to appreciate and find amusement in some of his unique ways of looking at things. We look forward to those infrequent occasions when he realizes he did something well and feels proud of himself. We are impressed when something temporarily opens a window and he writes a poem with clear insight.

Most important, these rare moments remind us that under all the problems and aggravations, there is a good kid who wants very much to be like everyone else. And that gives us the hope and strength to go on for one more day.

Andrew

My name is Jo Ellen, and I have a son with Asperger Syndrome. A year ago, I had never even heard of this syndrome, but now feel that I have tried to get my hand on every book, article, and piece of information that might help me understand my son and offer him the help that will guide him along in life. I am hoping that in writing down some of my thoughts and feelings, it might help other parents, families, friends, or teachers who are reaching out to the children who have Asperger Syndrome. Perhaps I can share some of the struggles and triumphs we have experienced with our son, Andrew, and perhaps in some small way help you through your journey.

Our son was diagnosed just a few months before his sixth birthday. My husband and I are educated professionals, he an engineer, and I a nurse. Andrew, the oldest child, lives with us and his 3-year-old sister in a middle-class suburban area. It has been only 7 months since we received the diagnosis, and a lot led up to it and a lot has happened since then. Actually, Andrew was one of the youngest children to be diagnosed with Asperger Syndrome, according to many professionals with whom we spoke. I worried that it meant he had a very severe case, but I think instead it was more our persistence and concerns that resulted in the diagnosis.

Andrew is a blond, blue-eyed boy who at age 6½ is a whiz on the computer and loves to look at science and experiment books. He attends an all-day kindergarten program in the public school system, and although he doesn't much like the schoolwork part, he already reads on the third-grade level. He looks like any other kindergartner; it isn't until you are around him more that you begin to notice subtle differences in his personality. For instance, he does not have much eye contact with other kids, and he is very particular about not touching finger paints or anything messy. He rarely raises his hand in school and often daydreams or gets a far-off look in his eyes. He has a hard time interacting with peers and occasionally screams out when he is upset. Lately, he has taken to a sort of self-talk to himself during quiet times, sort of "reliving" conversations with others. He is working on his knock-knock jokes, and we read books together on social situations. He doesn't play much with other children. He has to wear only sweatpants (because they are soft), he much prefers foods that go "crunch," and he won't eat slimy foods. We always thought he was the ideal child—he would always entertain himself so well when he was just a toddler. Little did we know that this was something that might be a sign of things to come.

I thought I would share some things that I have found helpful, at least for me, in working with a child with Asperger Syndrome. I will give a brief history up to diagnosis and then share some things that we as a family have found to be helpful.

Andrew was born 5 weeks early after a somewhat complicated pregnancy with preterm contractions. He spent a week in the neonatal intensive care unit because of a possible "seizure-like activity" that was proved negative with a CAT scan. He had no further neurological problems and seemed to develop well. He was slightly behind at the 9-month checkup on some motor skills, but with the premature birth adjustment, he was on target. He was a late walker—14 months—but talked right on schedule. His only real illnesses were frequent ear infections, which were treated with ear tubes. He always preferred to play alone, look at books, and entertain himself. Our friends said we had the "perfect child." He never was much of a climber, never tried to get out of his crib, and was always a good eater. He did, however, do things like line objects up according to size and shape, and he recognized unusual things in his environment, like the tape dispenser could be a number 6 or, when turned upside down, a 9. He began recognizing words at about age 3 to 4 and could put them in their proper context.

We did not have any concerns until Andrew started preschool at age 4. His teacher noticed that he couldn't put on his own shoes. She told us that she was worried about his self-esteem if he couldn't dress himself, but it didn't seem to upset him. She also said that he just was not "normal" like the other kids, that he didn't play with them much, and that his behavior went beyond "unique." Every phone call she made to us was negative, and after awhile I felt that she couldn't see anything positive about our son. After several phone calls to us about our child's "unusual behavior," she suggested we have him tested through the school system. We did as she requested, and they said he was "age appropriate."

As a mother I wanted to prove that Andrew was truly "normal," so I made an appointment with a developmental pediatrician at the nearby university medical center. The doctor there found him to be healthy and within normal limits; however, he was displaying something she called "opposition behavior"; that is, he was defying us and wouldn't dress himself. She suggested that we see a psychologist to help us with disciplining him.

We made an appointment with a behavioral psychologist, who worked with us on time-out procedures. This seemed to help some; he too could see how bright our son was. Andrew still couldn't dress himself very well, and we had many a frustrating morning trying to get the shoes on. After four or five sessions with the psychologist, he suggested we have our son tested for autism at a "multidisciplinary team screening." As a mother, I have to say that I was shocked. My son couldn't possibly have autism! Not my bright, wonderful son! What was this man suggesting, that my son had something major wrong with him?

The day of the testing I was more nervous than I thought possible. I told the speech therapist that I thought Andrew was tired, that he wouldn't perform well, that 3 hours in a row would tire him out, and that I wasn't comfortable with one test that would just label or diagnose him—just like that. She assured me that it would give us only information about how Andrew fit the autism spectrum and would show where he did or did not have problem areas.

They gave us the results at the summation conference, just an hour or so after all the tests were completed. Andrew was not autistic. I breathed such a sigh of relief. He did, however, have something called tactile defensiveness and dyspraxia (mild motor-planning problems). I learned that he was nearly 2 years behind on gross-motor skills, and 2½ years on daily living skills. I went from relief to fear to guilt. After all those mornings of coaxing him to put on his shoes and timing him out for not dressing himself, I learned that he didn't have the motor-planning ability to do it. Boy, did I feel bad as a mother and sad too—making him try to dress himself. The poor little guy was not developmentally able to do it. I also learned that with his tactile defensiveness he did not like messy things such as painting, touching gooey things, or even eating some slimy foods. We all came home exhausted.

The next step was trying to find appropriate help for him. I was disappointed in the testing site, as they were unable to provide me any therapy or treatment. They told me they were only a testing program, so I started calling occupational therapists listed in our phone book who worked with children. I found one who worked specifically with children, but due to insurance snags, we had to switch to another program. We were fortunate enough to have a children's hospital in the area and started with them. We have been very happy with the therapist there and have been visiting her for over a year now. She suggested that we retest Andrew for his gross-motor skills, so we had a physical therapist work with him. He was "age appropriate" after a summer of working on a few things like climbing the monkey bars, running, and jumping.

Andrew was now 5 and ready to start kindergarten; however, in light of his "problems," we decided to have him attend a pre-kindergarten class at a church-run preschool. The teacher was marvelous and made every effort to work with Andrew and us regarding our concerns. He was in a class with eight other boys and a certified teacher. He still didn't seem to play with the other children and often screamed out when a bright light would shine in his eyes. He rarely participated in the lessons, although he was easily reading all the books the teacher had. At recess he preferred to spend the time up in the lookout fort lost in his own thoughts. The teacher clearly could tell that he was bright; she just didn't know how to teach him.

In October we had his first parent–teacher conference, and the teacher said she continued to have concerns regarding how he was interacting with the class. She said he seemed very happy playing by himself on the playground or lost in his thoughts in the classroom. She already knew what we had done to date with his testing and therapy and was willing to help with anything that we suggested. I decided to call and see if he could be examined by another developmental pediatrician in town, but the wait was over 5 months. So in the interim we visited yet another behavioral psychologist, who worked with us on time-out again. They worked with Andrew and said he was pretty bright and that we should try more positive praise. They also suggested that we invite other children over, one at a time, and have monitored play sessions. We were to praise Andrew for playing appropriately and time him out when he didn't interact well with the other child. This was challenging, as Andrew only lasted about 10 minutes, and that left Dad or me to interact with the other child for the remainder of the session. We even contemplated trying medication for Andrew's hyperactivity at this time but decided to wait.

Our appointment with the developmental pediatrician finally arrived, and she was pleasant and very low-key. She took a thorough history from both my husband and myself, then worked with Andrew for a while. At the end of our session, she said she was not sure—in fact, could not be sure until further testing by a clinical psychologist was completed—but she felt that Andrew had Asperger Syndrome.

It was something we had never heard of. I felt great relief knowing that there was a physiological cause of some of Andrew's behaviors. Also, there was a deep sense of sadness—that I had lost my perfect little boy. I wanted to read everything. The doctor said that until the diagnosis was confirmed, she wanted me to read just one article. I remember taking it home, reading it from cover to cover, and saying, "Oh my God, that is Andrew." He didn't have some of the features some children with Asperger Syndrome have regarding memorizing dates, facts, or time schedules, but he always did like the United States map and could list most of the states. He definitely had trouble with eye contact and difficulty with social situations. These were his hallmark signs. He was hyperlexic and had some tactile defensiveness, which sometimes occur with Asperger Syndrome.

We were able to see the clinical psychologist within just a week, and she spent several hours with Andrew and me doing some paper-and-pencil tests and also some play therapy. She reviewed his history and asked me to return the next day with my husband, leaving Andrew at home. The next morning we went to her office, and she confirmed that our son had Asperger Syndrome. Now the tears started to flow. I remember her telling us that we would need to "change our expectations of Andrew." But what did that mean? I then envisioned my beautiful son living at home with us well into his 50s, never getting a job, never marrying—all due to this syndrome and to his inability to understand social rules and participate well in our very social world.

The doctor allowed me to be sad, mad, and frustrated all at the same time. She was very supportive and suggested several articles, and she also left the door open for support sessions for us as needed. To date, I see her every 6 to 8 weeks for ideas on how to deal with Andrew's behavior, problems that arise at school, and ideas on how to cope with our special needs child.

For over a year Andrew has met at least three times a month with an occupational therapist, who works with his motor planning and tactile defensiveness. She has him paint with shaving cream (which he hates), and she has him make up obstacle courses and tell her how he would execute his way through them (which he loves). She works really well with him, and I am happy to report that just this month, she felt he was age appropriate for most of the skills, for example, using scissors, writing with a pencil. We continue to work at home with the tactile kinds of things, and he has improved steadily.

We had to make the choice of having Andrew start in the public school system or in the parochial school where he was preenrolled for kindergarten. After talking with both schools, we felt that he would be entitled to more services and have a better chance of having his special needs met if we chose the local public school. We met with the school district, which just a few weeks before school started wanted to have Andrew take all kinds of intelligence tests, aptitude tests, and so on. He took them and did very well. The school district examiners were impressed with his excellent reading and comprehension skills but figured that his attention deficit might challenge the teachers. We were lucky that the school district had at least one other child with a diagnosis of Asperger Syndrome, so at least the administration understood some of what we were up against.

I met with the teachers Andrew would have. We selected the new all-day kindergarten program to lessen his need for transition and to provide continuity for him. We had to educate the staff about Asperger Syndrome, and they continue to work well with him and us as parents. The school had him tested with the occupational therapist on-site, but as expected, he did not qualify for therapy. However, he did qualify for their speech therapist to come into the classroom and work with him on conversational skills with the other children. She even brings games and has him teach another child how to play.

Andrew also started private speech therapy sessions before the school year started. I found a therapist who works well with pragmatics and social skills of speech, and she has helped him on a weekly basis. He likes the games she plays with him and is working on practical things like ordering a soda at McDonald's.

Another thing that I have found to be very helpful is talking with other parents whose children have Asperger Syndrome. When we received the diagnosis, I asked our developmental pediatrician to connect me with another mother who had recently gone through this experience of diagnosis and treatment. She found a very positive woman in our community who just 6 months before we met had received the diagnosis of Asperger Syndrome for her 10-year-old son. Her ideas, sharing, and support have really been a boost. Also, our community just happened to start a support group for parents of children with Asperger Syndrome. We meet monthly, share ideas and frustrations, and laugh at what other parents might be horrified to hear. It has been a wonderful sense of strength to see that the little oddities of your child are not so unusual and that other parents are going through the same kinds of things that you experience.

One thing that I have learned is that you have to grieve the loss of the perfect child. As parents, we all have expectations for our children. I always assumed that our son would be an engineer or scientist. I hoped that he would marry a nice girl and have a family. I don't know if any of these will come to pass; I hope that they all do. Right now, there are days that I am just thankful that we have had a calm day. He gets upset easily if he spills milk on his shirt or makes a mess of any kind. He cannot tie his own shoes (thank goodness for Velcro). He still gets frustrated with zippers and buttoning his own shirt. He is working on buttering his own waffles and cutting his own meat. It continues to be a struggle to get him to do any kind of art or to write. Andrew still has a hard time sitting still at mealtimes (but then again, don't most kids?).

Andrew rarely gets invited to anyone's house, and when he goes I worry about how he will act or react. He doesn't share toys well and doesn't understand the social skills that most 6-year-olds live by. He doesn't understand teasing and so is the victim of several classmates' pranks. It breaks a mother's heart to see her child be the butt of jokes, but you deal with it. Andrew doesn't understand humor very well, so we watch "America's Funniest Home Videos" on television and talk about why things are funny. We also have selected several knock-knock joke books to give him something to share with other people (and his teachers are great to laugh at his jokes). He has a hard time in new environments, so we try to explain everything as we go along. He isn't able to transfer social rules from one setting to the another, for example, "No kicking at school" can't be translated for him to "We don't kick at the playground." We have to remind him in each new setting of how to behave.

Parents deal with getting the diagnosis for a special needs child in different ways. You both start to feel guilty and wonder things like, "Did I give this to my child?" Both my husband and I tried to look back to our family trees to see if somehow we passed it down from generation to generation. Fathers grieve and accept in different ways from mothers—it must be in how we are genetically built. I'm not sure. I, as a mother, needed to grieve, to cry and talk it over with supportive family and friends. My husband, on the other hand, chose to be more self-reflective and to pursue the Internet for up-to-date information. Being in the health care field, I started reading all sorts of studies and technical articles. I wouldn't recommend them for most people, because they have a tendency to present the worst-case scenarios.

It is also hard to decide who you tell and how much they need to know. You would never want to hold back information from those caring for your child, but just how much you tell a neighbor or another child's parents is an individual call. Our families have been supportive and encouraging, and now that they know more of why Andrew gets upset easily or behaves the way he does, they are more accommodating and eager to help him excel in areas in which he can shine.

As I write this, Andrew is halfway through his kindergarten year. The school has 30-minute monthly meetings when we meet with teachers and the behavior specialist to discuss concerns or ideas regarding our son. They say he is doing better socially and has even initiated interactions with some of his classmates. He still doesn't raise his hand to answer questions and doesn't appear to follow a lot of the schoolwork. However, his reading skills are fine, and he has even participated in art class a little more. They do not think that he needs medication for the attention-deficit disorder at this time, and that is just fine by me. They also have started to let him have 20 minutes a day of computer time as a sort of motivational reward.

We continue to see the speech therapist weekly, and I keep a log for her of things to spark a conversation with Andrew. We have good communication with the school, and I am already planning ahead for the first grade.

Suggestions I have for someone who has a child with Asperger Syndrome are to keep an open mind and read all you can, especially handouts from your psychologist or therapists. Find someone you can confide in, like a sibling or best friend. These people are invaluable, as are any caring listeners. Spend one-on-one time with your child doing an activity he or she likes and excels at. It gives the child lots of positive reinforcement for things he or she already does well. Look up current sources on the Internet, in the library, or at autism centers. Start a parent support group in your area. It is really great to meet with other parents, and you might be able to help them as much as they help you. Truly, do not try to predict your child's future, just live in the present. Each child with Asperger Syndrome is different, and each child is special and unique. The most important suggestions I could give for parents, family members, teachers, or anyone working with these truly special needs children are to be patient, love them a lot, and celebrate their little victories.

Dan[*]

My son, Dan, is 21 and has Asperger Syndrome. We have traveled a long road to diagnosis and appropriate treatment. At times, discouragement seemed to overtake us, but we have gone farther now than we ever hoped. Our desire in telling Dan's story is that others will find hope and will determine never to give up!

Adopted at age 2½, Daniel was the joy of my life. When we got Dan, we were told that he had some developmental delays and might be mildly retarded. He wasn't speaking yet, had walked late, and was not potty trained. As a speech–language pathologist, I thought I could deal with those issues and more. He was so cute and seemed so needy. He was a perfect match!

Dan was not legally free for adoption. He had an unstable preadoption experience and had been in the foster care system for quite a while. However, parental rights had not yet been terminated. We agreed to take Dan as a foster child until he was free for adoption. The legalities went smoothly, and we eventually adopted Dan.

Dan had health and developmental difficulties from the beginning. The day after we brought him home, he started

---

*Adapted from "The Long Road," by Terri Carrington, 2000, *Focus on Autism and Other Developmental Disabilities, 15*(4), pp. 216–220. Copyright 2000 by PRO-ED, Inc. Adapted with permission.

crawling on the carpeted floor, scooting his ear along the rough carpet. He didn't cry or fuss, but he soon began to run a fever. Of course it was a weekend, and we had no pediatrician yet. We were able to take him to a friend's pediatrician, and he was diagnosed with an ear infection. Already his tympanic membranes were scarred and showed evidence of multiple infections. We checked with the adoption workers and found no evidence of prior treatment for ear infections. Dan had apparently found a way to soothe his ear by rubbing it on the carpet. This started a long course of chronic ear infections, antibiotic treatment, allergy treatments, insertion of tubes, and finally a prophylactic dose of antibiotic every day to curb the infections. Dan's lack of speech development and his clumsiness were attributed to the ear infections. We already had numerous concerns about his development, but the chronic ear infections seemed to explain the concerns away.

Dan's speech and language development was interesting. By the time we got him at age 2½, he had developed an elaborate gestural system interpreted by others fairly easily. The first word didn't come until age 4. He said "watch" and immediately began using it in kernel sentences with a variety of meanings: "Wear watch," "Watch TV," "Watch me." Curiously, he learned to read at about the same time. He loved books and was read to every day, but no formal attempt at teaching reading had been presented. By the time Dan entered kindergarten, he could read just about anything given to him. Speech continued to be problematic, and the diagnosis of dyspraxia was made. He had speech therapy privately and in school.

Dan's play skills were unusual, but because his play seemed so smart, red flags did not go up for us. He preferred constructive play to imaginative play and solitary play to group play. An activity he particularly enjoyed was lining up several wooden puzzles and then placing pieces one at a time and in the same place (e.g., left corner piece) in each puzzle down the line. When finished, he would dump the pieces, turn the puzzles to the side, and start the process over again. We thought he was so clever! Dan spent hours listening to Disney tape and book sets. He enjoyed doing this activity under a table or in some other small space. Electronic items and transportation were all-consuming interests. Dan also seemed to have an uncanny sense of direction. He loved spending hours with globes and maps and always received a new atlas for Christmas.

Emotionally there were also red flags, although we didn't see them at the time. Dan was affectionate, but indiscriminately so. He would go to anyone. He was as comfortable with a stranger in a grocery store as he was with us. He did show some separation anxiety when left at the church nursery or day care. I remember taking him to a Christmas parade where there was a homeless person sitting on the curb. Dan cuddled up to him as if they were long-lost friends. We didn't know what to do!

School was easy for Dan, at least in the academic sense. He was already reading and showing facility with numbers upon entering kindergarten. We went to a cemetery on Memorial Day that year, and Dan enjoyed walking along the rows of head-stones, reading people's names and figuring their ages at death. We were amazed. He continued to do well academically and was placed in the gifted and talented program in first grade.

School was a different story when it came to social issues. Dan had difficulty making friends, but he didn't seem bothered by it. We would have children over to play, but Dan tended to ignore them. We ended up playing with his friends! He was in Boy Scouts and Sunday school and participated marginally. We also tried several sports. Dan had undiagnosed sensory integration problems and visual problems (his eyes didn't converge), so the sports attempts were generally disasters. He almost always received the "most improved player" award, because he didn't have anywhere to go but up.

As Dan progressed in school, he became more and more disenfranchised with other students. He hated working in cooperative groups and going out for recess. He much preferred to spend his recess in the library with his books. Things were better for him at home. He rode his bike and then an all-terrain vehicle. We lived out in the country, and he seemed to enjoy that setting. We had a swimming pool, and Dan was a good swimmer. He enjoyed his time in the pool both by himself and with others.

About sixth grade, in a middle school setting, Dan began to deteriorate rapidly. He became obsessed with germs and developed compulsive behavior related to that. When someone would come too close, Dan would start blowing (to blow away germs). He wanted his clothes sterilized and would not wear underwear that someone else had touched. He became afraid of taking a bath and would cower at the end of the bathtub. Although we now know Dan was experiencing obsessive–compulsive disorder, sometimes seen in people with autism, we interpreted his behavior first as obstinance and then, as it increased in intensity, as paranoia.

By the time Dan reached seventh grade, he was frankly different from his peers, continued to engage in obsessive–compulsive thoughts and behaviors, and was performing poorly in school. A crisis ensued when Dan actually became fearful of his family, took the keys to one of our cars, and drove to a state south of us where we had often camped and vacationed. He managed to drive because he had used our riding lawn mower and his all-terrain vehicle, and we had let him occasionally drive our old truck in our field. He called when he ran out of gas, and we had him picked up by the police. When we arrived at the police station sometime later, we were blessed to deal with an experienced officer who recognized Dan's disorganization and knew something was wrong beyond a youth stealing a car. Dan was released back to our custody.

We contacted our pediatrician, who felt Dan should be hospitalized. This began a long road of dealing with the mental health system. Just a few years ago, autism wasn't recognized as the wide spectrum disorder it is, and Dan certainly did not fit the stereotypic image of a child with autism. The psychiatric hospitalization was lengthy and very scary. Autism was not considered as a diagnosis.

Because of Dan's foster care experience, resulting from parental neglect, and his current unexplainable behavior, Dan was thought to have reactive attachment disorder (RAD). We were unfamiliar with this disorder, but we read everything we could find. Children with RAD fail to bond with caregivers, usually because their early needs were not met. They fail to establish the cycle of bonding; where there is a need (such as a wet diaper or hunger), they let that need be known by crying and raging, and the need is then met. When early needs are not met, the foundational development of early building blocks such as cause and effect do not emerge. Without intensive and often controversial and intrusive treatment, development is skewed. These children are thought not to develop consciences, show no remorse, and are egocentric. They become manipulative and even dangerous. If not treated, children who display RAD may be diagnosed as sociopaths and psychopaths as adults—personality disorders thought to be resistant to treatment. We were told there was a poor prognosis for Dan; he would become progressively more dangerous, and he needed to be institutionalized. We reluctantly agreed for him to be placed in a residential treatment center following his hospitalization.

There can't be anything much worse than allowing your child to be placed somewhere other than the home. We weren't sure the placement would meet his needs and didn't feel comfortable with the facility. Unfortunately, it seemed the only answer at the time. Daniel did not do well there.

As we now know, he was misdiagnosed and received inappropriate treatment. He continued to deteriorate, running away from the facility. He found a small truck with keys in the ignition, took it, and drove to our property. The ordeal was terrifying, but there was nothing to do but return the truck and return Dan to the facility. With this scare, it seemed that staff at the facility would have watched Dan closely, as they were charged to do. Supervision was careless, and Dan took another vehicle—one of the facility vans—and drove it across state lines, was chased by the police, and rolled the van. Miraculously, he was not hurt. Later, the officers told me they expected a mean juvenile delinquent to emerge from the van. They were surprised when a chubby little kid with hard-to-understand speech and a poor understanding of what had transpired emerged from the van. Dan was jailed overnight, and we were again blessed with officers who allowed us to return Dan to our state. The staff at the facility and I retrieved Dan, and he was taken to juvenile detention. This was the first occurrence of what I call system dumping. When a child's behavior is unexplained or increases in difficulty, he or she often is dumped from one system or one facility to another. There didn't seem to be a framework for problem solving. If a child didn't fit, he or she was simply sent somewhere else. Fortunately, we were able to convince the juvenile authorities to rehospitalize Dan. During that hospitalization, I made an active search for a place that would meet Dan's perceived needs.

The diagnosis of RAD continued, and I found a facility in another state claiming to specialize in the disorder. By this time, we had exhausted the mental health provisions of our insurance policy. Because Dan is adopted, we were able to access adoption subsidy funding, which is negotiable and can be used in a variety of ways to meet a child's needs. Funding was provided for a 6-month stay at the new facility. Although the new facility seemed better than the first one, his treatment didn't seem adequate for the RAD diagnosis. He was not provided with the intensive treatment described in the literature for RAD, and the national consultant who was supposedly working with the facility never saw Dan. The psychiatrist who saw Dan, however, opened the door as to whether something "organic" was causing his symptoms. Unfortunately, this was not pursued. The recommendation continued to be that Dan had a poor prognosis and that he was probably facing a lifetime of institutionalization, if not imprisonment. In the meantime, Dan's father and I divorced, which left me to support Dan alone. I brought him home and enrolled him in school.

At his home school, Dan was placed in a behavior disorder classroom, which again did not meet his needs. This placement did not last long, and Dan found his way to yet another psychiatric hospitalization. Without detailing every hospitalization and placement, Dan eventually totaled 19 hospitalizations and 3 residential placements. Huge expenditures were required from the adoption subsidy, and a financial strain was put on me as well. The doctors and staff at these placements continued to misdiagnose and provide inappropriate treatment.

It was a long journey to the diagnosis of Asperger Syndrome. My own instincts as a speech–language pathologist, and the comments about Dan's status, seemed to say, "Look at autism." A friend who specialized in autism assessed Dan and felt he qualified for an educational diagnosis of autism in our state. Unfortunately, she wasn't taken seriously by the mental health community. At that time and in the place we lived, developmental disability professionals and agencies were reluctant to work with the mental health community, and vice versa. Children who displayed both mental health issues and developmental issues were in a no-man's land of sorts. Working together and sharing resources didn't happen. In fact, it seemed to me that the bottom line quite literally had to do with funding and wanting "someplace else" to pay the bill. It was fortunate that we had access to adoption subsidy funding. This funding source is negotiable and not tied to a program or diagnosis. Its use helped us cross agency and diagnostic lines. Through networking, I learned of a psychiatrist in a neighboring state who had expertise with developmental disabilities as well as psychiatric concerns. We obtained an evaluation from him—at my own cost, but worth it—which concluded that Dan not only qualified for an educational diagnosis of autism, but met the DSM–IV (*Diagnostic and Statistical Manual of Mental Disorders* [4th ed.]; American Psychiatric Association, 1994) criteria for Asperger Syndrome as well. Other mental health practitioners we had consulted at the time looked at Dan and expounded such things as, "He doesn't look autistic to me." Knowledge of autism spectrum disorders is increasing, but many clinicians continue to hold a narrow view of what autism "looks like."

The additional psychiatric report, coupled with the educational diagnostic report, supported our approach to the center for Mental Retardation and Developmental Disabilities, where Dan was accepted as a client. The Regional Center purchases services, and we were able to acquire the services of Pathways Supports, a company providing community integration, independent supported living, and psychological services. In fact, the psychologist with Pathways had provided services for Dan off and on for a long time and had been one of the few professionals who had remained supportive and open to our search for appropriate diagnosis and services. The staff at Pathways subscribes to the philosophy of positive behavior support. This same psychologist had been a member of the initial group of persons trained in positive behavior support in our state.

One of the tenets of positive behavior support is looking at individual needs and not limiting services to those suggested by a specific diagnosis or by what a particular agency is prepared to supply. Once needs are identified, an individualized program is designed to meet those needs. This was a breakthrough for Dan and our family. We were finally able to access what seemed to work for him. Before, we had been tied to whatever was available in his diagnostic box, whether that fit or not. Another tenet of positive behavior support was important to Dan's eventual success as well. The program was designed from the beginning to be dynamic and to change as Dan's needs changed. There were proactive plans for crisis intervention and plans to bring him back to original services if more intensive intervention was needed for a time. Other services, which were driven by placements made by diagnosis, ended when needs intensified. "Dan no longer fits our program" was the excuse as Dan hopped from placement to placement. There was no overall plan for Dan's cycles of needing increasing and decreasing levels of services. Each move was seen as a failure on Dan's part, when in fact the system failed to meet Dan's needs. The philosophy of positive behavior support places the child's needs first. Intervention services are tools to meet those needs. Success is measured not by ability to meet the requirements of an established program but by the child's meeting of individually established goals and objectives.

Because Dan was young, and because I wasn't willing to have him live anywhere except with me, we decided to provide an independent supported living arrangement in our home. This seemed workable, even though it was intensive. It certainly was better than institutional options. The road proved to be a rocky one. We initially had 24-hour staff with us. As time went on, the need for staff varied, from times with no staff present to times when we needed to double staff. During this time, my daughter also lived at home. She was in her late elementary–middle school career. In retrospect, the situation was difficult for her, although she did develop lifelong friendships with several of the staff members. When there is more than one child in a family, it is a never-ending balancing act to meet each one's needs even in the best of circumstances. When one child has needs that seem to far exceed the needs of another, life becomes challenging. She suffered as I made "Sophie's Choices" concerning both my children. One issue in particular continues to haunt me, and I have seen reference made to this in the adoption literature. When determining living choices for a very challenging child while considering arrangements for the other, more "normal" children, we need to consider safety paramount. My daughter was, at times, not safe in her own home. This is probably where a choice to provide services away from the home setting needs to be made, if possible. There were several instances where Dan's status deteriorated to the point that we made other arrangements—specifically, psychiatric hospitalization. These times were always difficult, but we were supported by the staff at Pathways. Dan was able to return to the independent supported living situation as his status improved.

There was, finally, a point when support in the home seemed no longer appropriate. It was time for Dan to move to an apartment. He was to be released from his latest lengthy psychiatric hospitalization, and the independent support living situation was moved. Although it was hard to let go, this proved to be the right choice. Dan's improvement was marked but continued to be marred by occasional crises. He eventually made a serious suicide attempt, which resulted in a broken femur. After the femur was repaired in surgery, Dan came home to stay with me and his sister. During his recovery, he again deteriorated, and it was determined that he again needed to leave home. The crisis was severe, and very clear lines were drawn in relation to Dan's living arrangements and our family. This seemed to be a turning point for Dan, and he has lived more or less successfully in supported living since. We continue to use the services of Pathways, but staffing has been reduced to a minimal level, and goals now focus on employment and community integration.

School has been a difficult issue. During Dan's elementary years, he excelled academically and seemed mostly oblivious to social demands. However, in junior high and high school, Dan's lack of social skills and his continuing speech disorder became more evident. Dan struggled and eventually turned school attendance into a daily battle. He finally refused to attend, and forcing him only escalated behavior difficulties. Homebound teaching was provided by the school, and one teacher provided some after-school work for Dan in the school building. The school provided minimal homebound services, because it is only reimbursed for a few hours a week. We eventually homeschooled and prepared Dan to take the test to obtain a general equivalency diploma (GED). He was not a wonderful home school student, but he took the test and scored well. He completed his GED during what would have been the fall semester of his senior year in high school. With that struggle over, we weren't willing to immediately look at postsecondary educational opportunities. (I think we do a nice job, for the most part, of educating and supporting our special needs elementary students. Unfortunately, when students transition to the secondary setting, problems occur for a variety of reasons. Increased academic demands, changing schedules, classes focused more on content than on students, lack of a safe place or home base, and lack of a peer group all contribute to decreased success.)

The student with Asperger Syndrome usually deeply wants to interact with others but lacks the skills and social perception to do so. Some students become so frustrated with their lack of social prowess that they actually become severely depressed. This certainly contributed to Dan's continuing mental health difficulties, as it does for many other students who function similarly. Furthermore, subtle language problems and continuing sensory issues compound the inability of these students to do well in school. Often their narrow focus of interest in a particular subject causes others to view them as very bright academically, so expectations are skewed. Sometimes alternative schooling options such as home schooling, enrollment in small private schools, or increased special education supports are beneficial. The most important aspect of these students' education is training for teachers and others who interact with the students so their needs relating to autism are identified and supported. Eventually, Dan tried two community college classes but felt he was unable to complete them. I was impressed, however, with the willingness of the faculty and support personnel to assist Dan. I hope we can try again.

Employment has not been as challenging as school completion. Dan has worked part-time for Pathways in a clerical position for several years. This has not been officially referred to as supported employment, but the nurturing environment at Pathways has contributed to Dan's success there. Asperger Syndrome is understood, and Dan's idiosyncratic behaviors have been tolerated, with his uniqueness even enjoyed by other workers. This experience has helped him establish confidence in his ability to work with others and has given him hope that he can be competitively employed. Currently, we are working with vocational rehabilitation to assist Dan in finding full-time competitive employment.

It has been a long road to diagnosis and appropriate services. As I think about the journey, it's appropriate to separate what worked and what did not. We need to look beyond the obvious. Dan's chronic otitis (ear infections) and early disrupted development were obvious explanations for his unusual behavior. If his behavior had been assessed in a systematic way, without preconceived ideas of cause, we might have looked further. The autism red flags were his disordered rates and sequence of development (facility with some developmental tasks and lags in others), his speech–language difficulties (dyspraxia, elaborate gestural system but no functional speech, late speech development that took an unusual course), early untaught reading, multiple sensory issues, narrow focus of interest, lack of facility with social skills, unusual play, more constructive than imaginative play, and superior intelligence as measured on standardized tests.

Many of the diagnosticians we consulted were not familiar with autism. They relied on their impressions and did not consider characteristics outlined in diagnostic guides. Furthermore, many clinicians did not consider that autism is a spectrum disorder and failed to recognize it in higher functioning individuals like my son.

There was a failure to consider the dual diagnosis of autism and mental health disorders. It is now my experience that many children have complex diagnoses and that children with Asperger Syndrome are at higher risk for mental health concerns such as depression and obsessive–compulsive disorder.

Practitioners were not willing to look beyond their own areas of expertise or the constraints of their employment setting. The mental health community did not work with the developmental disability and mental retardation agencies. There was an either-or philosophy. Diagnosis—whether appropriate or not—and funding sources drove treatment. Individual needs took a backseat to preset programs.

We took seriously the instincts that Dan's behavior had not been well explained over time. Hints from doctors that something organic was going on, and his resistance to treatment provided, indicated we were missing something. The addition of Asperger Syndrome to the DSM–IV and the additional outside evaluations I obtained gave credibility to our thoughts concerning autism.

Adoption subsidy funding, which is not tied to specific programs or agencies, was key in developing supports for Dan. Adherence to the philosophy of positive behavior supports by Pathways Supports and the Regional Center for Mental Retardation and Developmental Disabilities was central to developing appropriate services and to eliminating the hopping from program to program. Alternative schooling options were considered when traditional school enrollment was not appropriate.

As noted, Dan was eventually employed in a supportive environment. This has allowed him to develop confidence and ease in the search for competitive employment. The support of a few professionals, including Dan's adoption worker and the psychologist at Pathways who remained involved over time and through numerous crises, was critical to the overall continuity eventually achieved.

Recently, Dan spoke at the annual conference of the Autism Society of America. He did a great job outlining the long road he has walked. I think he gave hope for an eventual level of success for people with Asperger Syndrome. I have learned a great deal from Dan, as have the professionals who have chosen to support him. Being Dan's mom has been worth it!

Jason

Jason is an adolescent with a diagnosis of Asperger Syndrome. He shares here the original and unedited lyrics to a verse he wrote related to his experiences and frustrations in living with the daunting challenges of Asperger Syndrome. Jason also offers a perspective on his future. We end our book with this personal reflection on Asperger Syndrome because it so poignantly captures the significant emotional and other challenges connected with this disability. At the same time, it reflects the optimism that we have found so common among children and families with Asperger Syndrome. We firmly believe that, with the assistance of qualified and committed professionals and knowledgeable and resolute parents and families, individuals with Asperger Syndrome will be able to actualize their significant potential and live productive lives, both as students and adults.

Doomed from a Cause Unseen[*]

I got cuffs to my wrists and shackels on me.
My life really twists like the waves of the sea.
I'm a living rage, my fist like flail,
Im an innacent prisoner in a cell.
I got some nuckels and some nasty scenes
where some heads fly clear to New Orleans
but theres an evil shadow that holds the key
to the evil chains that strongly bind me.
He clung to me I didnt cling to him
cause he ticks me off every time he clings to my skin

---

*Poem reprinted with permission of the author.

but Im not going to let him ruin my life
I got to raise some kids I got to get a wife.
Im going to be someone, maybe someone to lead
but my detirmination weighs a ton and I will succeed.
These ratling chains weigh heavy on my soul
but my desperation glows like a flaming coal.
Im getting back up, Im breaking out of this cage.
I shake the bars hard to express my rage.
I rise in my shackels back up again.
I yell outloud in my torcher pin.
I bash to the left and I bash to the right
Im not giving up without a fight.
I got a painful past but a life ahead.
I hope you heard just what I said.
I got a painful past behind my back
but a life ahead that I cant keep slack.

References

American Psychiatric Association. (1994). *Diagnostic and statistical manual of mental disorders* (4th ed.). Washington, DC: Author.

American Psychiatric Association. (2000). *Diagnostic and statistical manual of mental disorders* (4th ed., text revision). Washington, DC: Author.

Americans with Disabilities Act of 1990, 42 U.S.C. § 12101 *et seq.*

Arwood, E. L. (1991). *Semantic and pragmatic language disorders* (2nd ed.). Denver, CO: Aspen.

Asperger, H. (1944). Die 'Autistischen Psychopathen' im Kindesalter. ["Autistic Psychopathy" in Childhood]. *Archiv fur Psychiatrie und Nervenkrankheiten, 117,* 76–136.

Attwood, T. (1998). *Asperger's Syndrome: A guide for parents and professionals.* London: Jessica Kingsley.

Autism Society of America. (1995). Definition of autism. *Advocate, 27*(6), 3.

Ayres, A. J. (1989). *Sensory Integration and Praxis Test.* Los Angeles: Western Psychological Services.

Barnhill, G. P. (2001). Social attribution and depression in adolescents with Asperger Syndrome. *Focus on Autism and Other Developmental Disabilities, 16,* 46–53.

Barnhill, G., Hagiwara, T., Myles, B. S., & Simpson, R. L. (2000). Asperger Syndrome: A study of the cognitive profiles of 37 children and adolescents. *Focus on Autism and Other Developmental Disabilities, 15,* 146–153.

Barnhill, G. P., Hagiwara, T., Myles, B. S., Simpson, R. L., Brick, M., & Griswold, D. (2000). Parent, teacher and self report of problems and adaptive behaviors in children and adolescents with Asperger Syndrome. *Diagnostique, 25,* 147–167.

Baron-Cohen, S., Leslie, A., & Frith, U. (1985). Does the autistic child have a theory of mind? *Cognition, 25,* 37–46.

Baron-Cohen, S., O'Riordan, M., Stone, V., Jones, R., & Plaisted, K. (1999). Recognition of faux pas by normally developing children and children with Asperger Syndrome or high-functioning autism. *Journal of Autism and Developmental Disorders, 29,* 407–418.

Bieber, J. (Producer). (1994). *Learning disabilities and social skills with Richard LaVoie: Last one picked . . . first one picked on* [videotape]. Available from Public Broadcasting Service Video, 1320 Braddock Place, Alexandria, VA 22314.

Brigance, A. H. (1980). *Brigance Diagnostic Inventory of Essential Skills.* North Billerica, MA: Curriculum Associates.

Bruner, J. S. (1966). *Toward a theory of instruction.* Cambridge, MA: Harvard University Press.

Carlson, J. K., Hagiwara, T., & Quinn, C. (1998). Assessment of students with autism. In R. L. Simpson & B. S. Myles (Eds.), *Educating children and youth with autism: Strategies for effective practice* (pp. 25–54). Austin, TX: PRO-ED.

Carpenter, L. B. (2001). The Travel Card. In B. S. Myles & D. Adreon (Eds.), *Asperger Syndrome and adolescence: Practical solutions for school success* (pp. 92–96). Shawnee Mission, KS: Autism Asperger Publishing Company.

Carrington, T. (2000). The long road. *Focus on Autism and Other Developmental Disabilities, 15*(4), 216–220.

Cesaroni, L., & Garber, M. (1991). Exploring the experience of autism through firsthand accounts. *Journal of Autism and Developmental Disorders, 21,* 303–313.

Church, C., Alisanski, S., & Amanullah, S. (2000). The social, behavioral, and academic experiences of children with Asperger Syndrome. *Focus on Autism and Other Developmental Disabilities, 15,* 12–20.

Conroy, M., & Fox, J. J. (1994). Setting events and challenging behaviors in the classroom: Incorporating contextual factors into effective intervention plans. *Preventing School Failure, 38,* 29–34.

Dolch, E. W. (1955). *Methods in reading.* Champaign, IL: Garrard Press.

Downing, J. A. (1990). Contingency contracts: A step-by-step format. *Intervention in School and Clinic, 26,* 111–113.

Duffy, M. L., Jones, J., & Thomas, S. W. (1999). Using portfolios to foster independent thinking. *Intervention in School and Clinic, 35,* 34–37.

Duke, M. P., Nowicki, S., & Martin, E. A. (1996). *Teaching your child the language of social success.* Atlanta, GA: Peachtree Publishers.

Dunn, W. (1999). *The Sensory Profile: A contextual measure of children's responses to sensory experiences in daily life.* San Antonio, TX: Psychological Corp.

Dunn, W., Myles, B. S., & Orr, S. (2002). Sensory processing issues associated with Asperger Syndrome: A preliminary investigation. *American Journal of Occupational Therapy, 56*(1), 97–102.

Durand, V. M., & Crimmins, D. (1992*). Motivation Assessment Scale.* Topeka, KS: Monaco & Associates.

Durrell, D. D., & Catterson, J. H. (1981). *Durrell Analysis of Reading Difficulty* (3rd ed.). San Antonio, TX: Psychological Corp.

Ehlers, S., & Gillberg, C. (1993). The epidemiology of Asperger Syndrome: A total population study. *Journal of Child Psychology and Psychiatry, 34*(8), 1237–1350.

Ehlers, S., Nyden, A., Gillberg, B., Sandburg, A., Dehlgren, S., Hjelmquist, E., & Oden, A. (1997). Asperger Syndrome, autism and attention deficit disorders: A comparative study of cognitive profiles of 120 children. *Journal of Child Psychology and Psychiatry and Allied Disciplines, 38,* 207–217.

Frith, U. (Ed.). (1991). *Autism and Asperger Syndrome.* Cambridge, UK: Cambridge University Press.

Fry, E. B. (1980). The new instant word list. *The Reading Teacher, 34,* 284–289.

Gable, R., Hendrickson, J. M., & Sealander, K. (1997). Eco-behavioral assessment to identify classroom correlates of students' learning and behavior problems. *Beyond Behavior, 8*(2), 25–27.

Gagnon, E. (2001). *The power card: Using special interests to motivate children and youth with Asperger Syndrome and autism.* Shawnee Mission, KS: Autism Asperger Publishing Company.

Ghaziuddin, M., Weidmer-Mikhail, E., & Ghaziuddin, N. (1998). Comorbidity of Asperger Syndrome: A preliminary report. *Journal of Intellectual Disability Research, 42*(4), 279–283.

Gillberg, C. (1989). Asperger Syndrome in 23 Swedish children. *Developmental Medicine and Child Neurology, 31,* 520–531.

Gillberg, C. L. (1992). Autism and autistic-like conditions: Subclasses among disorders of empathy. *Journal of Child Psychology and Psychiatry and Allied Disciplines, 33,* 813–842.

Gillberg, I. C., & Gillberg, C. L. (1989). Asperger Syndrome—Some epidemiological considerations: A research note. *Journal of Child Psychology and Psychiatry and Allied Disciplines, 30,* 631–638.

Gilliam, J. E. (2001). *Gilliam Asperger Disorder Scale.* Austin, TX: PRO-ED.

Goldstein, A. P., & McGinnis, E. (1997). *Skillstreaming the adolescent: New strategies and perspectives for teaching prosocial skills.* Champaign, IL: Research Press.

Grandin, T. (1995). *Thinking in pictures and other reports from my life with autism.* New York: Vintage.

Gray, C. (1994, October). *Making sense out of the world: Social stories, comic strip conversations, and related instructional techniques.* Paper presented at the Midwest Educational Leadership Conference on Autism, Kansas City, MO.

Gray, C. (1995). *Social stories unlimited: Social stories and comic strip conversations.* Jenison, MI: Jenison Public Schools.

Gray, C., & Garand, J. D. (1993). Social stories: Improving responses of students with autism with accurate social information. *Focus on Autistic Behavior, 8,* 1–10.

Griswold, D., Barnhill, G. P., Myles, B. S., Hagiwara, T., & Simpson, R. L. (2002). Asperger Syndrome and academic achievement. *Focus on Autism and Other Developmental Disabilities, 17*(2), 94–102.

Guber, P., Peters, J. (Producers), & Levinson, B. (Director). (1988). *Rain Man* [Motion picture]. (Available from MGM/UA Home Video, 2500 Broadway, Santa Monica, CA 90404-3061)

Guerin, G. R., & Maier, A. S. (1983). *Informal assessment in education.* Palo Alto, CA: Mayfield.

Hagiwara, T., & Myles, B. (1999). A multimedia social story intervention: Teaching skills to children with autism. *Focus on Autism and Other Developmental Disabilities, 14,* 82–95.

Harn, W. E., Bradshaw, M. L., & Ogletree, B. T. (1999). The speech–language pathologist in the schools: Changing roles. *Intervention in the School and Clinic, 34,* 163–169.

Hendrick-Keefe, C. (1995, Winter). Portfolios: Mirrors of learning. *Teaching Exceptional Children, 27,* 66–67.

Howlin, P., Baron-Cohen, S., & Hadwin, J. (1999). *Teaching children with autism to mind-read: A practical guide.* New York: Wiley.

Hudson, F. G., Colson, S. E., & Braxdale, C. T. (1984). Instructional planning for dysfunctional learners: Levels of presentation. *Focus on Exceptional Children, 17*(3), 1–12.

Hudson, F. G., Colson, S. E., & Welch, D. L. H. (1989). *Hudson Education Skills Inventory.* Austin, TX: PRO-ED.

Johnson, B. A. (1996). *Language disorders in children: An introductory clinical perspective.* Boston: Delmar.

Joliffe, T., & Baron-Cohen, S. (1999). The strange stories test: A replication with high-functioning adults with autism or Asperger Syndrome. *Journal of Autism and Developmental Disorders, 29,* 395–406.

Jones, V. F., & Jones, L. S. (1995). *Comprehensive classroom management: Creating positive learning environments for all students* (4th ed.). Boston: Allyn & Bacon.

Kadesjo, B., Gillberg, C., & Hagberg, B. (1999). Autism and Asperger Syndrome in seven-year-old children: A total population study. *Journal of Autism and Developmental Disorders, 29,* 327–332.

Kamps, D. M., Leonard, B. R., Dugan, E. P., Boland, B., & Greenwood, C. R. (1991). The use of ecobehavioral assessment to identify naturally occurring effective procedures in classrooms serving students with autism and other developmental disabilities. *Journal of Behavioral Education, 1,* 367–397.

Kanner, L. (1943). Autistic disturbances of affective content. *The Nervous Child, 2,* 217–250.

Kaplan, J. S., & Carter, J. (1995). *Beyond behavior modification: A cognitive–behavioral approach to behavior management in the school* (3rd ed.). Austin, TX: PRO-ED.

Klin, A., Sparrow, S. S., Marans, W. D., Carter, A., & Volkmar, F. R. (2000). Assessment issues in children and adolescents with Asperger Syndrome. In A. Klin, F. R. Volkmar, & S. S. Sparrow (Eds.), *Asperger Syndrome* (pp. 309–339). New York: Guilford Press.

Klin, A., Volkmar, F.R., & Sparrow, S. (2000). *Asperger Syndrome.* New York: Guilford Press.

Kuttler, S., Myles, B. S., & Carlson, J. K. (1998). The use of social stories to reduce precursors to tantrum behavior in a student with autism. *Focus on Autism and Other Developmental Disabilities, 13,* 176–182.

Lewis, T. J., Scott, T. M., & Sugai, G. (1994). The problem behavior questionnaire: A teacher-based instrument to develop functional hypotheses of problem behavior in general education settings. *Diagnostique, 19,* 103–115.

Lincoln, A., Courchesne, E., Kilman, B., Elmasian, R., & Allen, M. (1988). A study of intellectual ability in high-functioning people with autism. *Journal of Autism and Developmental Disorders, 18,* 505–524.

Lord, C., & Venter, A. (1992). Outcome and follow-up studies of high-functioning autistic individuals. In E. Schopler & G. B. Mesibov (Eds.), *High-functioning individuals with autism* (pp. 187–199). New York: Plenum Press.

MacLeod, A. (1999). The Birmingham community support scene for adults with Asperger Syndrome. *Autism, 3,* 177–192.

Manjiviona, J., & Prior, M. (1995). Comparison of Asperger Syndrome and high-functioning autistic children on a test of motor impairment. *Journal of Autism and Developmental Disorders, 25,* 23–39.

Mawhood, L., & Howlin, P. (1999). The outcome of a supported employment scheme for high-functioning adults with autism or Asperger Syndrome. *Autism, 3,* 229–254.

McIntosh, D. N., Miller, L. J., Shyu, V., & Dunn, W. (1999*). Short Sensory Profile.* San Antonio, TX: Psychological Corp.

McLaughlin-Cheng, E. (1998). Asperger Syndrome and autism: A literature review and meta-analysis. *Focus on Autism and Other Developmental Disabilities, 13,* 234–245.

Mercer, C. D. (1996). *Students with learning disabilities* (6th ed.). Columbus, OH: Prentice Hall.

Michael Thompson Productions. (2000). *Social language groups.* Naperville, IL: Author.

Moran, M. R. (1982). Language development and language disorders. In E. L. Meyen (Ed.), *Exceptional children in today's schools: An alternative resource book* (pp. 91–118). Denver, CO: Love.

Moran, M. R. (1995). *Teacher assessment for instructional planning.* Unpublished manuscript.

Myles, B. S., & Adreon, D. (2001). *Asperger Syndrome and adolescence: Practical solutions for school success*. Shawnee Mission, KS: Autism Asperger Publishing Company.

Myles, B. S., Bock, S. J., & Simpson, R. L. (2000). *Asperger Syndrome Diagnostic Test*. Austin, TX: PRO-ED.

Myles, B. S., Constant, J. A., Simpson, R. L., & Carlson, J. K. (1989). Educational assessment of students with higher-functioning autistic disorder. *Focus on Autistic Behavior, 4*, 1–13.

Myles, B. S., Cook, K. T., Miller, N. E., Rinner, L., & Robbins, L. A. (2000). *Asperger Syndrome and sensory issues: Practical solutions for making sense of the world*. Shawnee Mission, KS: Autism Asperger Publishing Company.

Myles, B. S., & Simpson, R. (2001a). Effective practices for students with Asperger Syndrome. *Focus on Exceptional Children, 34*(3), 1–14.

Myles, B. S., & Simpson, R. L. (2001b). Understanding the hidden curriculum: An essential social skill for children and youth with Asperger Syndrome. *Intervention in School and Clinic, 36*(5), 279–286.

Myles, B. S., Simpson, R. L., & Becker, J. (1995). An analysis of characteristics of students diagnosed with higher-functioning autistic disorder. *Exceptionality, 5*(1), 19–30.

Myles, B. S., & Southwick, J. (1999). *Asperger Syndrome and difficult moments: Practical solutions for tantrums, rage, and meltdowns*. Shawnee Mission, KS: Autism Asperger Publishing Company.

Norris, C., & Dattilo, J. (1999). Evaluating effects of a social story intervention on a young girl with autism. *Focus on Autism and Other Developmental Disabilities, 14*, 180–186.

Phelps-Terasaki, D., & Phelps-Gunn, T. (1992). *Test of Pragmatic Language*. Austin, TX: PRO-ED.

Piaget, J. (1959). *Judgment and reasoning in the child*. Paterson, NJ: Littlefield, Adams.

Quinn, C., Swaggart, B. L., & Myles, B. S. (1994). *Focus on Autistic Behavior, 9*(4), 1–13.

Reisman, F. K. (1972). *A guide to the diagnostic teaching of arithmetic*. Columbus, OH: Charles E. Merrill.

Reynolds, C. R., & Kamphaus, R. W. (1992). *Behavior Assessment System for Children (BASC)*. Circle Pines, MN: American Guidance Services.

Rinner, L. (2000). *Asperger Syndrome and autism: Comparing sensory processing in daily life*. Unpublished master's thesis, University of Kansas, Lawrence.

Roberts, G. H. (1968). The failure strategies of third grade arithmetic pupils. *The Arithmetic Teacher, 15*, 442–446.

Rogers, M. F., & Myles, B. S. (2001). Using social stories and comic strip conversations to interpret social situations for an adolescent with Asperger Syndrome. *Intervention in School and Clinic, 36*, 310–313.

Rumsey, J. M. (1992). Neuropsychological studies of high-level autism. In E. Schopler & G. B. Mesibov (Eds.), *High-functioning individuals with autism* (pp. 41–64). New York: Plenum Press.

Safran, S. (2001). Asperger Syndrome: The emerging challenge to special education. *Exceptional Children, 67*, 151–160.

Schutt, P. W., & McCabe, V. M. (1994). Portfolio assessment for students with learning disabilities. *Learning Disabilities Quarterly, 5*, 81–85.

Semel, E., Wiig, E. H., & Secord, W. A. (1995). *Clinical Evaluation of Language Fundamentals* (3rd ed.). San Antonio, TX: Psychological Corp.

Shure, M. B. (1992). *I can problem solve: An interpersonal cognitive problem-solving program*. Champaign, IL: Research Press.

Siegel, D., Minshew, N., & Goldstein, G. (1996). Wechsler IQ profiles in diagnosis of high-functioning autism. *Journal of Autism and Developmental Disorders, 26*, 389–406.

Silvaroli, N. J. (1986). *Classroom Reading Inventory*. Dubuque, IA: Wm. C. Brown.

Skrtic, T. M., Kvam, N. E., & Beals, V. L. (1983). Identifying and remediating the subtraction errors of learning disabled adolescents. *The Pointer, 27*, 323–338.

Smith, I. (2000). Motor functioning in Asperger Syndrome. In A. Klin, F. Volkmar, & S. Sparrow (Eds.), *Asperger Syndrome* (pp. 97–124). New York: Guilford Press.

Smith, I., & Bryson, S. (1994). Imitation and action in autism: A critical review. *Psychological Bulletin, 116*, 259–273.

Sparrow, S., Balla, D., & Cicchetti, D. (1984). *Interview edition of the survey form manual: Vineland Adaptive Behavior Scales*. Circle Pines, MN: American Guidance Service.

Spivack, G., Platt, J. J., & Shure, M. (1976). *The problem-solving approach to adjustment*. San Francisco: Jossey-Bass.

Stanford, P., & Siders, J. A. (2001). Authentic assessment for intervention. *Intervention in School and Clinic, 36*, 163–167.

Sundbye, N. (2001). *Assessing the struggling reader: What to look for and how to make sense of it*. Lawrence, KS: Curriculum Solutions.

Sundbye, N., & McCoy, L. J. (1997). *Helping the struggling reader: What to teach and how to teach it*. Lawrence, KS: Curriculum Solutions.

Swaggart, B. L., Gagnon, E., Bock, S. J., Earles, T. L., Quinn, C., Myles, B. S., & Simpson, R. L. (1995). Using social stories to teach social and behavioral skills to children with autism. *Focus on Autistic Behavior, 10*(1), 1–16.

Swicegood, P. (1994). Portfolio-based assessment practices: The uses of portfolio assessment for students with behavioral disorders or learning disabilities. *Intervention in School and Clinic, 30*, 6–15.

Szatmari, P. (1991). Asperger's syndrome: Diagnosis, treatment, and outcome. *Psychiatric Clinics of North America, 14*, 81–93.

Thorndike, R. L., Hagen, E., & Sattler, J. (1985). *Stanford–Binet Intelligence Scale* (4th ed.). Chicago: Riverside.

Volkmar, F., & Klin, A. (2000). Diagnostic issues. In A. Klin, F. Volkmar, & S. Sparrow (Eds.), *Asperger Syndrome* (pp. 25–71). New York: Guilford Press.

Volkmar, F., Klin, F., & Cohen, D. (1997). Diagnosis and classification of autism and related conditions: Consensus and issues. In D. J. Cohen & F. R. Volkmar (Eds.), *Handbook of autism and pervasive developmental disorders* (pp. 5–40). New York: Wiley.

Wallace, G., & Hammill, D. (1994). *Comprehensive Receptive and Expressive Vocabulary Test*. Austin, TX: PRO-ED.

Wechsler, D. (1989). *Wechsler Preschool and Primary Scale of Intelligence–Revised*. San Antonio: Psychological Corp.

Wechsler, D. (1991). *Wechsler Intelligence Scale for Children* (3rd ed.). San Antonio, TX: Psychological Corp.

Wetherby, A., & Prizant, B. (2000). *Autism spectrum disorders: A transactional developmental perspective*. Baltimore: Brookes.

Wiig, E. H., & Secord, W. (1989). *Test of Language Competence–Expanded Edition.* San Antonio, TX: Psychological Corp.

Wilde, L. D., Koegel, L. K., & Koegel, R. L. (1992). *Increasing success in school through priming: A training manual.* Santa Barbara: University of California.

Williams, K. (2001). Understanding the student with Asperger Syndrome: Guidelines for teachers. *Intervention in School and Clinic, 36,* 287–292.

Winebrenner, S. (2001). *Teaching gifted kids in the regular classroom: Strategies and techniques every teacher can use to meet the academic needs of the gifted and talented.* Minneapolis, MN: Free Spirit.

Wing, L. (1981). Asperger's Syndrome: A clinical account. *Psychological Medicine, 11,* 115–130.

Wing, L. (1991). The relationship between Asperger's Syndrome and Kanner's autism. In U. Frith (Ed.), *Autism and Asperger Syndrome* (pp. 37–92). Cambridge, UK: Cambridge University Press.

World Health Organization. (1992). *International statistical classification of diseases and related health problems–Tenth revision.* Geneva, Switzerland: Author.

Zachman, L., Barrett, M., Huisingh, R., Orman, J., & Blagden, C. (1991). *Test of Problem Solving–Adolescent.* East Moline, IL: LinguiSystems.

Zachman, L., Huisingh, R., Barrett, M., Orman, J., & LoGiudice, C. (1994). *Test of Problem Solving–Elementary, Revised.* East Moline, IL: LinguiSystems.

Index

About the Authors

Brenda Smith Myles, associate professor in the Department of Special Education, codirects a graduate program in autism spectrum disorders at the University of Kansas. She has authored numerous books and articles on autism and Asperger Syndrome and has lectured internationally on this topic. Myles is also the editor of the journal *Intervention in School and Clinic.*

Richard L. Simpson is professor of special education and school psychology at the University of Kansas and acting director of special education programs at the University of Kansas Medical Center. He has worked as a special education teacher, school psychologist, and clinical psychologist. He is senior editor of the professional journal *Focus on Autism and Other Developmental Disabilities.*